Liberalism & How it's Destroying America

By

I0440716

Mark Phillips

TABLE OF CONTENTS

PREFACE

Preface

If you are reading this book, the odds are you're not a liberal. The book's title alone would turn off most liberal democrats. What you will read is what I like to believe is some eye opening information about many of the hot political topics of the day. The war on terror, illegal immigration – yep they're both here. I shine the light on liberal hypocrisy, from our elected officials, the dinosaur media as well as from the limousine liberals living out in Hollywood. I discuss the topics with a mixture of hard facts and satirical humor.

Satire is a very effective tool to discuss what can be very complicated topics. I use it to both introduce a level of lightheartedness while driving some very serious points home. For example, I refer to Rosie O'Donnell as a noted metallurgist as a way to point out the idiocy of her comment that steel doesn't melt. This was part of her assertion that 9/11 was an inside job. I'd love for her to tell us exactly where the steel beam farms are where this stuff grows out of the ground ready to be put into buildings.

I also cover many of the important issues that have real consequences for everybody as Americans. So, in light of that I also take a serious look at many of these issues. I discuss the liberals' desire to surrender in Iraq, our Nation's failure to control illegal immigration and more. The mixture of satire and hard facts will arm you with the information needed to fight the arguments of the left, while at the same time being what I hope will be a fun read.

Chapter #1

Liberals and the War on Terror

We are in the midst of an epic fight, one that will define what our world will look like for our children and our children's children. We are facing a very determined enemy. Islamo-facists mean to destroy everybody that is different than they are. Make no mistake this is not a live and let live benevolent ideology. Iran is the chief sponsor of terrorism around the globe. Al-Qaeda, along with what have been called affiliated terrorists organizations want the entire world ruled by Sharia law. Calling Sharia law strict and brutal would be an incredible understatement. Arab men have been put to death for the crime of shaving off their beards. News flash for the left, these guys aren't too high on equal rights for women either.

A History of Intolerance

According to the left, George W. Bush is the reason that Islamic terrorists are angry with us. It is his policies that have angered them, and they would adopt a live and left live philosophy if not for Bush. The truth is that the United States has been dealing with middle-eastern terrorists throughout our entire nation's history. Barbary pirates were attacking American trading vessels going back to the days of George Washington. As Washington's Secretary of State, Thomas Jefferson traveled to the middle-east to see if a diplomatic solution could be reached. He was told that the Arabs considered us infidels, and were not interested in peace with us. Jefferson was told that they believed that if they were to die fighting us, they would be rewarded in death with 72 virgins. Now, the Europeans opted to pay off the Arab pirates instead of fighting them. This is akin to protection money that cowed business owners in Chicago would pay Al Capone. As president, Jefferson ordered a military attack against the Barbary pirates rather than agreeing to bribe them. This fact is recounted in the Marine Corp hymn. *"From the Halls of Montezuma, to* **the shores of Tripoli**", thus immortalizing the battle.

Interestingly enough, Keith Ellison Democrat Congressman from Minnesota opted to take the oath of office by placing his hand on Thomas Jefferson's Koran, and not the bible as is tradition. As the first Muslim elected to the U.S. congress, he did this to show that Jefferson had enough respect for Islam to own a copy of the Koran. The particular copy was translated into English by George Sale. Sale wrote a message in the book, warning us of the dangers that Muslims pose to the West, thus making this an interesting choice for Ellison to use.

The Religion of Peace

If the Islamic radicals could nuke every Jew and Christian right now, they would. Even moderate Muslims are not exempt from their hatred. I find it interesting that to a lot of liberals, it's President Bush and conservative Republicans that are the real threat to the world, and not the terrorists. The left will speak more harshly about Rush Limbaugh and Ann Coulter than they do of Mahmoud Ahmadinejad. I wonder if they ever stop to consider how progressive the terrorists are on issues such as; equality for women, gay rights, freedom of speech, freedom of the press (Hugo Chavez), and other social issues?

We'd better come to grips with the level of determination that we're dealing with. Most westerners myself included, have a very hard time understanding a level of fanaticism that would lead a young man to strap a bomb to his body and blow himself up in a disco or an outdoor market place just to kill innocent civilians. Most of us love life too much and just don't hate that deeply. Even if I could find that level of hate in my heart, as a parent, I certainly couldn't send my own child out to blow himself up. Yet, for Palestinians such suicide bombing attacks against Israelis are common place. Many are taught to hate and to seek martyrdom starting early in life in the public schools. When grade school age children dress up as mini-suicide bombers during graduation we're talking about a very dedicated enemy. We are dealing with an enemy that is far more dedicated to their cause than apparently we are to ours. When the stakes are this high that is not a good thing.

Suicide bombings are not limited to a small minority of radicals that only represent a fringe of Muslim society. A poll taken in May, 2007 by the Pew Research Center showed that 26% of Muslims living in the United States thought that suicide bombings were ok. Let that sink in for a moment, a quarter of the Muslims living here in America think that strapping a bomb to your body and blowing up civilians is acceptable behavior. I am by no means of the mind set that all Muslims are fanatic killers. Far from it, the silent majority are in fact peaceful people who just want to go about their daily lives just like you and me.

What I do find troubling is that they are in fact silent. The vocal fanatical minority are painting a picture that they're all nothing but a bunch of bloodthirsty middle-evil lunatics.

Where are the protests from the 'average' Muslim condemning the horrors that are being unleashed on the world in the name of their religion? If only moderate Muslims would take to the streets and march with the same passion as illegals do. Also keep in mind that most Germans were not Jew slaughtering Nazis. The sad truth is that a radical minority can thwart the will of a silent majority. Good hearted Germans didn't act, and the horrors of Nazism were unleashed upon the World.

A Palestinian Homeland

The Palestinians want a homeland that they can call their own. This sounds fine on the surface. Upon further assessment however, this benign request starts to take on a more sinister tone. The Palestinians were offered a homeland in 1948, the same year that Israel was offered theirs. They refused, and opted instead, along with several other Arabs counties, to go to war with Israel. The 'plight' of the Palestinian's becomes even more ludicrous when you consider the actual size of the nation of Israel in relation to the rest of the middle-east. As the map below shows, Israel is a very small nation surrounded by countries, most of which that would just as soon see it wiped off the face of the Earth. The repeated 'land for peace' deals that the Palestinian's 'agree to' are a farce that Israel should stop making. Since giving the Palestinians the West

Bank, Israel now have enemies on all sides. This is not an enviable position militarily speaking.

Aside from that point, in the name of solidarity, when was the last time you heard any of the Arab countries in the middle-east offering land for the Palestinians to call their own? A big mistake that both democrat and republican administrations have made is to try and convince Israel to give in to just one more Palestinian demand in exchange for lasting peace. Making concessions to terrorists does promote peace, it only encourages more terrorism.

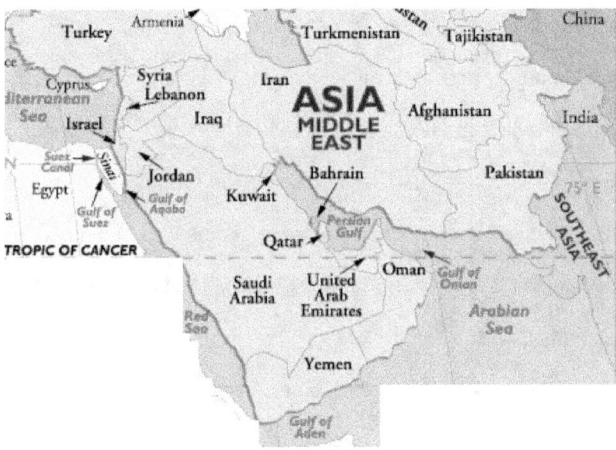

Keeping your eye on the Ball

Liberal democrats love to say how President Bush took his eye off the ball by attacking Iraq. Al-Qaeda was based in Afghanistan, and the response to the 9/11 attacks should have started and finished there. It would be like condemning

President Franklin Roosevelt for committing U.S. military forces to the European theatre during World War II. After all, it was Japan that attacked Pearl Harbor on December 7th, 1941. He obviously took his eye off the ball by not focusing solely on Japan. While both Germany and Italy did declare war us, they hadn't fired a shot single shot against us prior to our engaging in the European conflict. Iran is killing more American soldiers now, than German or Italy did prior to our sending troops into Europe.

President Roosevelt engaged in acts of military aggression against those two sovereign nations that had not attacked us first. I guess it wasn't Bush that first attacked a sovereign country preemptively. Perhaps world renowned foreign policy guru Jimmy Carter should read up on his history a little more. Remember, this is the man that didn't support the Shah, and thus allowed Iran to be taken over by Islamic radicals. His next stroke of foreign policy genius was sit on his hands while the same nuts that took over Iran held our citizens hostage for 444 days. Hint to the left, Jimmy Carter is not the guy to listen to for sound advice on how to deal effectively with terrorists. This is the same Jimmy Carter that has called the administration of George W. Bush the worst in U.S. history.

Airport Security

A little known truth is that we did have policies in place that might have kept at least some of the Al-Qaeda hijackers from boarding the airplanes on 9/11. Some of the hijackers arrived last minute, purchased first class tickets with cash, and didn't have any luggage with them. Up to about a year prior to 9/11, these actions would have been considered suspicious and subjected the hijackers to additional security scrutiny. Maybe, just maybe they wouldn't have been permitted to board the airplanes that faithful day. We can thank liberals and organizations like the ACLU for forcing airlines to drop these types of practices. In fact, if an airline dares to focus on Arab males, the ACLU will be screaming racism and decrying the evils of racial profiling. I travel a fair amount in my job, and just when I thought that I had seen it all, a TSA airport security screener did something astonishing. Now, it is not unusual for them to pick shapely young women to be subjected to the x-ray machines that can see through clothing. No Arab males, but plenty of cute young ladies. During my latest flight, I actually saw a TSA security screener scrutinizing a young kid's stuffed Garfield. What was getting dangerously close to a body cavity search was a stark reminder that the government is not focusing its resources on making air travel safer.

The hard truth is that for the good of our country, we better darn well start racial profiling. We are at war with Islamo-Fascists, the overwhelming majority of which are males of Arab descent. Now, I'm not advocating that we place all Arabs males that are currently in the country in internment camps. That would be wrong, just as it was wrong for President Franklin Roosevelt to place Japanese Americans in internment camps during World War II. While discussed more in the chapter on illegal immigration, I believe that we should put an immediate moratorium on all immigration from Arab countries. That would include student visas, work visas, everything. We're at war and such a policy while it would inconvenience a certain amount of honest hard working Arabs, it would likely keeps hundreds of hardened terrorists and terrorist wannabees out of the country.

Modern Day Iran – Jimmy Carter's gift to the World

This once relatively pro-western nation is now a major sponsor of terrorist activities around the world. Hezbollah and Hamas are Iranian proxies. Iran is sending troops and weaponry into Iraq to kill our soldiers. By any reasoned account, these are acts of war. Germany and Italy declared war against us, but hadn't attack us prior our sending troops into Europe. Iran hasn't publicly announced they're at war with us, but they are attacking us. Which scenario is more worthy of an American military response? We need to be very clear here, present day Iran is the Nazi Germany of our day. Ahmadinejad is more dangerous because he's trying to get access to weapons that didn't exist in Hitler's time. Of course, according to Keith Ellison, democrat congressman from Minnesota, President Bush is no better than Adolf Hitler. I wish that I could say that Ellison, the first Muslim elected to Congress, holds a uniquely radical view. However, where are the other democrats condemning his comments? I'm no fan of Bill Clinton, but I wouldn't compare his administration to Hitler. A more accurate comparison would be to Hugh Hefner perhaps but certainly not Hitler.

When Adolf Hitler wrote Mein Kampf from inside of his prison cell, he was very open about the horrors he planned to unleash upon the world if given the opportunity. Well he was and he did. Ahmadinejad has stated that if he ever gets a nuclear bomb that he will destroy Israel. I know this much, if I were the Israelis I would take that threat very seriously. Iran considers Israel a little Satan, a puppet of the United States whom they consider the great Satan. We can't afford to underestimate the dangers of a nuclear Iran. I fully believe that *if Iran is permitted to obtain a nuclear weapon, they will use it.* While the cold war was certainly no cake walk, at least Soviets were in touch with reality enough to be deterred by what was called mutually assured destruction. Iran is so out of touch with reality, that if given the chance, they will drop a nuclear bomb on the United States. Never mind that we have enough weaponry to wipe them off the face of the planet. Remember these guys seek martyrdom.

According to the left, we need to engage in open dialogue with Iran to rise above our disagreements and form partnerships. News flash for the left, Ahmadinejad doesn't want peace with the United States, he wants to destroy us. Where exactly are we supposed to begin a meaningful dialogue with a man who is so out of touch with reality that he believes that the holocaust never happened? Any promises that Iran makes won't be worth the paper that they're printed on. They'll be just as effective as the promises North Korea made back in 1994 concerning their nuclear weapons ambitions. While stating the obvious to anybody to the right of John F'n Kerry, no amount of United Nations sanctions will have an effect on Iran either. We've had a trade embargo against Cuba for over 40 years now. While grandpa Fidel has destroyed the economy of Cuba, hasn't modified his leftist policies one iota. North Korea is also dirt poor, and that government has built a nuclear bomb. If Iran is not stopped, they will build a nuclear weapon and they will use it. Of course to San Fran Nan, the real threat to America is the conservative Christian white male.

While Iran is rich in oil, they don't have any refineries necessary to turn the oil into gas. If we were to stop any gas from going into Iran, their automobiles would come to a dead halt in short order. So, no worthless decades of U.N. liberal non-sense, but real pressure including the real threat of military action may help deter Iran from their nuclear weapons ambitions. Air strikes against their nuclear facilities should be on the table as well.

Arabs Don't Want Democracy or Freedom

It has been argued that Sunni and Shia will never co-exist due to their long history of fighting each other. Perhaps, in the long run Iraq will be divided into three semi-autonomous states with a single centralized government. Quasi self rule with revenue sharing of the county's oil revenues may ultimately be the future for Iraq. For those who think that a democratic government will never work in the middle-east, bear in mind that until the United States came along, no nation had ever had a successful democracy. Also bear in mind that Iraqi voter turn out for their post-Saddam democratic elections was over 80%. It sounds like at least some Iraqis are warming up to the idea of a democratically elected government. This is even more incredible when you consider that many Iraqis literally risked their lives in order to vote.

Also bear min mind that much of the difficulties facing Iraq today is not Shia/Sunni infighting. It is Al-Qaeda terrorists as well as Iranian insurgents that are causing the majority of the violence in Iraq. How effective would our nation have been in 1791 if we had to fight a war on our soil while still a fledgling democracy?

I also find it interesting that is the as so tolerant left that says something so obviously racist as to assert that Arabs can't handle democratic self-rule. Perhaps liberals think that all Arabs are capable of are hatred and murder. An interesting position from a supposedly tolerant ideology. I wonder if in the mind of left wing democrats, Pakistan's President Musharraf, Afghanistan's Hamid Harzai and Iraqi President Jalal Talabani are not any better than Mahmoud Ahmadinejad.

Perhaps what is truly a shame is that by all counts, the Arab cultures should be the most advanced in the world. These are the people that were building pyramids 5,000 years ago. The sad truth is what should be a highly advanced culture has allowed itself to be taken over by extremism. Instead of leading the world into the 21st century, they have opted to live in the dark ages.

9/11 was our Fault

It's been suggested that our own actions around the world is what caused the terrorists to attack us on 9/11. Even if that position was true, Al-Qaeda began planning their 9/11 attacks during the 1990's. Is the liberal left saying that it was the policies of Bill Clinton that angered the terrorists? The terrorists will not adopt a live and let live policy if we were to withdraw from the world. In fact, just the opposite is true. They would interpret such an action as a show of weakness and be emboldened. This is exactly what happened in the 1990's when President Clinton failed to perform his Constitutional responsibilities as commander-n-chief and respond appropriately when faced with repeated acts of war against Americans.

Left wing foreign policy genius Rosie O'Donnell has said that the American troops have killed hundreds of thousands of Iraqis, making us the real terrorists. News flash to Miss O'Donnell – Hussein killed more Iraqi's during his brutal rule than have died as a result our military action in the Iraq war. The United States also goes to great lengths to minimize civilian casualties. If the terrorist were truly angry because Arabs were being killed, they would have deposed Hussein years ago. Saddam gassed Kurds by the thousands. For those of you on the left, that's using weapons of mass destruction. We don't destroy their Mosques, they do. If anything, we show both their people and their religion more respect then they do.

It is also worth stating that there is almost no country in the world today that the United States hasn't helped out in times of need. The American people are the most generous and giving people in the history of mankind. We have freed millions of people from fascism, communism, Nazism and more. As we're trying to free millions from the awful grip of terrorism, it would nice if liberalism wasn't getting in the way. Also remember that there is no nation on earth that has used it military might with as much restraint as we do. We did not take over half of Europe after World War II like the Soviets did. We liberate we do not conquer.

Those that don't Learn from History are Damned to Repeat It.

Does any serious person with even a minimal understanding of history think that America getting involved in Europe during World War II wasn't a good idea? Germany and Italy were two very dangerous nations at that time. They were brutal beyond comprehension, and were hell bent on world domination.

They also didn't have a real love for Jews, especially Hitler. Back then, we realized that the threat that Germany and Italy posed was a global threat. It was in America's best interest to get involved and to do whatever we could to stop the insanity. Bear in mind that Roosevelt was certainly no right-wing republican. This was a liberal democrat who understood these dangers well enough to realize the need for strong military action against both Germany and Italy.

World War II was entirely avoidable. If the free nations of the World had taken action against Hitler without waiting for him to build up the German military, millions of lives would have been saved. Winston Churchill urged England to take action against Hitler in 1936. Neville Chamberlain opted instead to seek peace with der Furor, and the rest as they say is history. I wonder if liberals still think letting Iran get a nuclear bomb is a good idea. As of 2007, estimates for Iran actually getting a nuclear bomb range anywhere from 2 years to 10 years. So, how close do we let Iran get before we take the threat seriously? What ever we do, let's not send Joe Wilson out to investigate this.

Thoughtful people can disagree on a whole slew of social issues. However, ignoring the threat of terrorism is down right suicidal. Like many of you, I am a big fan of the Fox News Channel show Hannity & Colmes. (Well - mainly the Hannity part) I was quite surprised when Alan Colmes stated that the Bush administration shouldn't complain about a Hugo Chavez type because we're always trying to promote democracies and he's the democratically elected leader of Venezuela. Adolf Hitler was the lawfully elected leader of Germany. Would Alan argue that since he was lawfully elected, that we shouldn't have opposed him? Mahmoud Ahmadinejad is the duly elected leader of Iran. Should we not oppose him even though he is definitely at war with us? Again, liberals have complained about the hawkish war stance of the right. Perhaps Fox News should run video of the 9/11 attacks on a daily basis to remind people of the horrors that terrorist have in store for us. Actually, there are two problems with that idea. First of all, most of the people that watch the Fox News Channel already understand the threat that terrorists pose. Secondly, showing video of the 9/11 attacks would certainly only hasten the passing of the kill conservative free-speech bill. In D.C. they call it the Fairness Doctrine.

We Need a Strong President

Muammar Gaddafi of Libya declared his 'Line of Death' across the Gulf of Sidra in 1986, warning that he would destroy any U.S. forces that dared to cross it. He basically stated that what was drawing a line in the sand (or in the water) in violation of treaties with regards to what is classified as international waters. Reagan responded as the true leader he was. He used American airpower and bombed several military targets in Libya. The result of Reagan's decisive action was that we haven't had a problem with this two-bit dictator since. In fact, once President Bush started his war against terrorism, Gaddafi voluntarily gave up his program to acquire weapons of mass destruction. Having strong leaders in the White House does make America and the rest of the world safer. Now, let's look at the other side.

Since Carter's pathetic handling of the 1979 Iranian hostage crisis, the terrorists are convinced we're nothing but a paper tiger without the will to use our military might. Listening to the democratic presidential candidates debate, I'd have to agree with them. When asked what they would do if we were attacked on our own soil, and we knew who did it, most responded how they'd make sure FEMA had their act together. OK – if I'm a terrorist any one of those democrats is getting my vote. Consider the attacks against the United States during the Clinton administration. The 1993 World Trade Center bombing, the attack on the U.S.S. Cole, the Khobar Towers and more, none of which elicited a meaningful military response from our then command-n-chief. If it weren't for the Lewinsky affair, he never would have ordered the bombing of the aspirin factory in the Sudan.

While democrats are lambasting Bush on how he is conducting the war on terror, he at least is doing something. Remember, there hasn't been a successful terrorist attack on our soil since 9/11. This is not by accident. Juxtaposition that with Clinton's lack of any response which only served to embolden the terrorists, culminating in the 9/11 attacks. Sudan offered Bin Laden up to Clinton numerous times during the 1990's, and he wanted no part of it. This is the person that the liberals consider a great president. Heaven help us is Mrs. Bill Clinton becomes president.

Liberal democrats have stated that our response to the 9/11 attacks has been disproportional. It would be like saying that after we killed 2400 Japanese soldiers we should have called it even for their attack on Pearl Harbor. Perhaps we should have limited our response to the December 7th attacks to retaliating against their naval armada. After all, Hitler no more attacked Pearl Harbor than Hussein flew airplanes into the twin towers.

Towards the end of the war in the Pacific, Japan knew they couldn't defeat us militarily. They also knew that they didn't have to, and could still win the war. As America was planning on invading the Japanese mainland, they knew that they only had to inflict enough casualties to make us give up. They didn't have to defeat our soldiers, just break our political will. President Truman knew this as well. It was one of the reasons he decided to drop two atomic bombs on Japan rather than invading their soil. By any account, it was the toughest decision of his presidency. The Japanese loss of life at Hiroshima and Nagasaki were almost all civilian. Civilian casualties in a time of war are both tragic and unavoidable. As a civilized nation should we try to minimize the loss of life of civilian non-combatants in war time? The obvious answer is that of course we should. Bear in mind that in this present conflict, our enemy doesn't care about sparing civilian life. They use civilians as human shields, and hide out in Mosques. The terrorist are killing more Muslims and destroying more Mosques that any American or European forces.

Remember that Saddam Hussein killed more Iraqis then the coalition forces have. He was brutal beyond comprehension. So when Ted Kennedy stated that Abu Ghraib was still open, just under new management to insinuate that the U.S. military was just as brutal as Saddam was truly disgraceful. Was what a handful of U.S. soldiers did wrong – yes. However, it didn't raise the level of brutality that Saddam practiced. It certainly wasn't sanctioned by either the

U.S. military or the Bush administration. So, Senator Kennedy either knows that, and is lying for political advantage with the loony left, or is truly out of touch with reality. In short, he's either lying or delusional. Of course, I don't have high expectations of the champion of Chappaquiddick. If anything, I wonder just how many women he has to drown before the Massachusetts liberals stop re-electing him to the Senate.

Then of course there's our base in Guantanamo where we house terrorist prisoners of war. I find it interesting that we make the effort to provide them culturally sensitive food. They brutalize and behead our captured soldiers, and we provide them with culturally sensitive food. You know what 'f' the culturally sensitivity menu crap. Those bastards can eat ham sandwiches for all I care. Perhaps we should put Maricopa Country Sheriff Joe Arpaio in charge of feeding them. Bologna sandwiches all around. That's pork bologna and not the all beef variety.

"The War is Lost", or so proclaimed Senator Harry Reid (democrat from Nevada) on April 19th, 2007. This is no 'obscure' unknown U.S. senator, if there even is such a thing. Mr. Reid is the Senate Majority Leader. To help ensure that we did loose the war on terror, the democrats tried to set firm dates for surrender. Make no mistake, whether it's called withdrawal, redeployment or bringing the troops home, setting a date like that during a war is just about as stupid a thing as possibly can be done militarily. It tells our enemy, just hide out for a couple of months, and the American troops will leave on their own. If we had told Hitler that the Americans would leave Europe on a specific date in 1945, World War II would have had an entirely different outcome. If we had Mrs. Bill Clinton, Harry Reid and Nancy Pelosi back then, today our national anthem would be Deuchland Uber Alles.

Of course, we all know the tremendous success the 1994 accords with North Korea were. We give them oil and technology, and they 'promised' not to build nuclear weapons. Oops, ok they did build nuclear weapons. I guess we need to once again thank prominent foreign policy guru Jimmy Carter. Perhaps we should impose economic sanctions on North Korea. History tells us that they had a tremendous impact on Iraq. While 'suffering' under the pressures of the U.N. sanctions poor old Saddam built dozens of presidential palaces for himself and his two sadistic sons. Hint to the liberal left, dictators don't give a damn about economic sanctions. They don't care about the welfare of their citizenry. Take a look at an aerial photograph of North Korea. With the exception of the capital where Kim Jong III lives, the country is completely in the dark. (Literally and figuratively). Perhaps if Danny Glover needs more funding for his movies than his good buddy Hugo Chavez can come up with, he can approach Kim Jong III.

Serious Penalties for Early Withdrawal

Wars don't always go as planned, in fact they never do. They're messy, civilians get killed, and property gets destroyed. War is something any sane person would avoid at almost all cost. Make no mistake, the opposite of war is not peace, sometimes the opposite of war is loss of freedom and death. The democrats want us to believe that if we just pulled out of Iraq, that all would be fine, peace in our time. If we pull out of Iraq before that country can defend itself, Al-Qaeda, the Iranians and other terrorists will swarm in and destroy the new Iraqi democracy. When we pulled out of Vietnam abruptly, the North slaughtered millions of South Vietnamese. Again, we need to learn from the lessons of history. If we pull out of Iraq now, millions of Iraqis will be slaughtered. Iran would solidify its stance as the main power of the middle-East. America will loose its credibility around the world. It will be a long time before any country will want to join a coalition with the United States to combat terrorism.

Interestingly enough, we have more than ample military might to win the war in Iraq. It's the political will that we lack. The terrorist know that they can't defeat the United States military, they don't have to. They just have to hang in there long enough cause enough pain and the democrats will send our brave troops packing. Due to the chaos and carnage that was involved in D-Day, there isn't an exact count on the number of casualties the United States suffered that day. However, we lost more troops on June 6, 1944 during the D-Day landing, than we lost in all of 2006 fighting the war on terror. I will say of course that as an American, every U.S. casualty is one too many. I make this point to illustrate the fact that the terrorist are not defeating us militarily. Hell, more Americans are killed each year by drunk drivers than in military action in Iraq. You don't see liberals decrying that our highways are lost to drunks. By some counts the terrorists have been reduced from 9/11 type attacks to being dependent on Iran providing them IEDs and other weaponry to kill our troops. We've caused sufficient disruption to keep them from launching successful attacks on our soil. Note to Bill Clinton – that's what a commander-n-chief is supposed to do.

It is also worth noting that Iraq has drafted a Constitution, held several free elections, they have built schools and hospitals and more. Are things going as well as we would like over there? Of course not. Mistakes have been made, but perhaps President Bush's job would be a little easier if in addition to trying to fight a war, he didn't have to fight liberal democrats doing everything they can do to loose the war for us.

Noted military strategist Walter Cronkite declared that the Vietnam War was lost after the North's 1968 Tet offensive. Militarily, the offensive was not successful for the North and the United States military was not defeated. Politically, with the help of Mr. Cronkite, we lost the political will to fight. I can't leave a discussion about the Vietnam War without mentioning Jane Fonda, a traitor to the American people. Hanoi Jane is at it again protesting against the war on terror. She's apparently not satisfied with having the blood of dead U.S. soldiers in Vietnam on her hands. She wants her irresponsible acts to cause American military deaths in the present time as well.

Just for the record, before the polls and organizations like MoveOn.org drove them to change their positions, both Al Gore and Mrs. Bill Clinton repeatedly stated that Saddam was a threat that had to be dealt with. They've since flip/flopped for political reasons. What would our world be like today if Roosevelt decided in 1943 that Germany and Italy weren't really all that bad and decided not to enter the European theatre?

Iraq & Weapons of Mass Destruction

Liberals love to say how President Bush misled the country by stating that Iraq had weapons of mass destruction. Saddam killed tens of thousands of Kurds by using poisonous gas. As a friendly reminder to liberals, poisonous gas is a weapon of mass destruction. Several bombs containing Sarin and Mustard Gas have also been discovered in Iraq by United States military. A centrifuge, which is a part needed to build a nuclear bomb, was uncovered as well. Did we find the huge treasure trove that everybody believed Saddam to have? The answer is no. However, with the months of advanced warning that he was given, he could have boxed up his WMD materials and trucked them into Syria. I doubt that in 2003 Saddam truly expected to be permanently removed from power. He sure as hell didn't expect a new Iraqi government to execute him for war crimes against his own people. He probably thought that he would hide out for a year or two, and return to power. With the possible exception of Rosie O'Donnell, Saddam was probably the most disappointed person on the planet that John Kerry didn't win the 2004 presidential election. Had Kerry been elected, Hussein would very likely be back in control of Iraq today.

Al-Qaeda Rebuilding

There are reports that Al-Qaeda is rebuilding in the mountainous region that borders Afghanistan and Pakistan. The terrain is very difficult to move in, and neither government is either willing or able to exert control over the area.

The resulting lawlessness would be a haven for terrorism. Rather than let Al-Qaeda regain strength, a desolate mountainous region sounds like a very good candidate for some real American air power. If there is in fact credible evidence that Al-Qaeda is using that area to rebuild, and the two governments aren't doing anything about it, the United States should take decisive action. If Afghanistan and Pakistan can't flush out Al-Qaeda, we should drop some major ordnance (bombs) on the terrorist training camps. I'm talking about a whole bunch of MOABS (mother of all bombs) and more. Level the damn place. For those that say that such a statement is harsh, keep in mind that during World War II, the drive to purchase war bonds was often accompanied by the slogan that said something to the effect - to allow our troops to rain bombs on the Nazis. It would be a danger to our national security if we were to allow Al-Qaeda safe haven anywhere around the globe. If Mrs. Bill Clinton or any democrat is elected president in 2008, Al-Qaeda will have all the safe havens that hey need. The ones that are in this country already would likely be given amnesty. Democrats can not be entrusted with something as serious as our national defense. To be fair, there are in fact a very select group of democrats that do understand the seriousness of the terrorist threat. Zell Miller and Joe Lieberman are very rare amongst today's democrats. In fact Zell Miller is so disappointed in today's democrat party that he wrote a book entitled "A National Party no More". Lieberman actually lost the democratic primary to be re-elected to his senate seat. He actually chose to run as an Independent, and won. Apparently the broader population of voters in Connecticut are more in touch with reality than those that vote in the democrat primary. Lieberman was Gore's vice-presidential running mate in 2000, and it took nothing more than to break with the radical left's stance on the war to have him loose his primary bid to be re-elected for his senate seat. When Lieberman lost the primary, whacko leftists such as Michael Moore and the MoveOn.org crowd warned other democrats that they would suffer his fate if they dared to break with them on this issue. The extreme left exerts far too much influence on today's democrats. This party really needs to find its soul again, or as Zell might put it, become a National Party again. It was fun to see the left go silent when Lieberman won as an Independent.

Chapter #2

Hollywood's Dramatic Move to the Left:

Hollywood today is a bastion of left-wing lunacy. Notice that I said Hollywood today – and not just Hollywood. There was a time when the values of actors more closely mirrored those of the rest of society. I'm not saying that 50 years ago they were indistinguishable from the makeup of the National Rifle Association. However, how many actors besides Charlton Heston would proudly admit to being a member of the NRA? Successful actors have always had an abundance of wealth, beyond what the rest of us can probably fathom. Yet, they weren't always these extreme leftist totally disconnected from reality that they are today. Now, in all fairness, not all Hollywood types liken to the philosophies of Michael Moore and Rosie O'Donnell. However, today's liberals are so intolerant many of the more moderate ones don't dare speak out in fear of damaging their careers. Yes, liberals are the intolerant ones not conservatives.

The Golden Age

Hollywood hasn't always been dominated by left-wing radicals. In fact, looking back at the World War II era, some of our Nation's biggest heroes were famous actors. Audy Murphy was the most decorated soldier in all of World War II. Yes – that is the same Audy Murphy who was also a very famous Hollywood actor. Other notable actors that were also military veterans include names such as; James Doohan, Bob Keeshan (Captain Kangaroo), Jimmy Stewart, David Niven, Don Adams, Bob Barker, Ernest Borgnine, Charles Bronson, Mel Brooks, Johnny Carson, William Conrad, Jackie Coogan, Kirk Douglas, Buddy Ebsen, Tony Curtis, Charles Durning, Norman Fell, Glenn Ford, Bill Holden, DeForest Kelly, George Kennedy, Werner Klemperer, Jack Klugman, Ted Knight and Don Knotts. Yep – good old Barney Fife himself. He had more than just one bullet in his shirt pocket while serving in the military. While the list of names I've just rattled off is long, it is by no means comprehensive as there are in fact many more actors who were also military veterans. However, I listed the number that I did to illustrate the point that at one time, there were actually a large number of patriotic Americans working as actors in Hollywood.

I want to name two more Hollywood actors that while not veterans, were great patriots in their own rights. Bob Hope, a hugely successful actor did just incredible work in supporting the troops. Bob Hope put on shows for the American G.I. in every conflict that the United States was involved in from World War II to Desert Storm. He supported the American soldier. His volunteer work on behalf of the troops was truly inspiring. Finally, it wouldn't be right to have a discussion about actors that were American patriots without mentioning John Wayne. The Duke was perhaps the biggest star of his day, and certainly a true patriot. If the Duke were alive today, what words would he have for Mr. Moore? That is an exchange I'd like to see.

Today's Hollywood

Fast forward from World War II to today and consider the names that I've listed above with personalities such as; Rose O'Donnell, Susan Saradon, Danny Glover, Sean Penn, Charlie Sheen and more. To these Hollywood lefties, George W. Bush is more of a terrorist than Osama Bin Laden or Mahmoud Ahmadinejad. Rosie O'Donnell has said that Christians are just as bad as Islamo-facists. The last time that I checked, Christians are not going around beheading Muslims. When I go to church, which is not as often as I should, I have never heard the Priest advocate violence. Neither Jewish nor Christian religious schools teach their students to dress up as suicide bombers to murder civilians. I have yet to hear one serious religious leader from either Judaism or Christianity support beheading people in the name of their religion. In fact, for both Jews and Christians, one of God's commandments states that you shall not murder.

Of course to left wingers like O'Donnell, conservative Christians are perhaps the biggest threat to the world. Hey Rosie, the last time I checked, it was your beloved Islamic extremists that want to deny women the right to vote, don't give them any access to education, and basically treat them like second class citizens. Rosie has it pretty good in this country. She's shrill, abrasive, certainly not a gorgeous hunk of female, and yet this country has given her the opportunity to allow her to become rich, and famous. The worst thing a white republican like me would do against Rosie is to not watch any television show she's on, and not go to any movie she stars in.

I do have to admit that from time to time I would watch her on the View. It was mainly out of morbid curiosity that I liken to people slowing down in order to get a better view of a serious car crash. Again, let me state that I don't promote censorship, and actually enjoy a good thoughtful debate. With that said, Rosie's arguments were rude, shrill and grossly uninformed. I truly felt sorry for many of her co-hosts. At best, Rosie monopolized the show bringing it down to her uniformed extreme leftist level. At worst she personally attacked anybody on the View that dared to disagree with her. At one point she said that people didn't like her because she was an overweight lesbian. Actually, I find her lack of serious intellect and anti-American views repulsive. Like most conservatives, I am more thoughtful than to care that she may not be the most beautiful woman in the country today. Katie Couric is an attractive female. I don't watch her on T.V. either because of her non-sense liberal biased views.

Hollywood Intellectual Lightweights

Rosie stated that poor ole' Khalid Shaikh Mohammed, the Al Qaeda terrorist, who was captured back in 2003, had been in U.S. custody since 1993. O.K. so she was only 10 years off. She also showed a photo of Khalid looking somewhat a mess, to show what years of torture at the hands of evil white conservative Americans can do to a guy. The photo that she was referring to was taken shortly after he was captured, and before he was actually in a United States facility. Hey Rosie, for the record he looks like crap naturally. She actually looked a lot like the now famous photo of Khalid Shaikh Mohammed when she was demonstrating how she hangs upside down to relax. There were two more flaws in Rosie's 1993 statement. For one, Clinton had no interest in capturing Al Qaeda terrorists. That was a job left to his successor. Secondly, had Khalid

Shaikh Mohammed been captured in 1993, was she insinuating that he had been tortured under Clinton's watch?

Sean Penn actually traveled to Iraq before the United States invaded it. He wanted to see for himself if Saddam's government was as bad as he was hearing from the right. For the record, the left (Clinton, Kerry etc.) were pretty anti-Saddam at that point in time too. So, members of Saddam's government greeted this incredibly naive actor, using him as the propaganda puppet that his is. So, upon his return Sean Penn gleefully stated what a nice guy Saddam was, and how much his people loved him. Earth to Sean Penn, did you expect him to take you to one of his rape rooms, or let you watch as he had one of his citizens put through a wood chopper? Perhaps a tour of the mass graves filled with dead Kurds? Sean Penn was just about as effective in his overseas trip as Joe Wilson was in his.

Another Hollywood icon is left-wing lunacy is Danny Glover. He has embraced Hugo Chavez of Venezuela (literally). Chavez is going to finance Glover's movie making endeavors to the tune of approximately 20 million dollars. This is the same Hugo Chavez that while addressing the United Nations general assembly compared President Bush to the devil. Now, I am no big fan of former President Clinton. However, as an American I would not want to hear him publicly bad mouthed by the leader of another country. So, here you have a two-bit nutty dictator that is in the process of destroying Venezuela denouncing the leader of the greatest country the world has ever known. This is the person that Danny Glover has the love feast with. I can't help but wonder why a hugely successful actor like Glover has to seek funding from a nut like Chavez. Is the movie that he wants to produce so bad that nobody in the states wants to support it?

I miss the days when a democrat President actually didn't embrace ruthless dictators. John F. Kennedy had no love for Fidel Castro. It would be nice if the Kennedy's of today had half the common sense that he did. Joe Kennedy nephew of the late president should perhaps not embrace good ole' Hugo Chavez so much. What would John F. Kennedy and Harry Truman think of today's democrats?

Extremism as Mainstream

It would be one thing if these liberal fanatics were a fringe group that people dismissed. However, unfortunately this is not the case. Michael Moore, one of the most extreme leftist actually sat with former President Jimmy Carter during the 2004 Democrat Convention. While at the convention, Mr. Moore the political mental pigmy that he is stated that *". . . supporters of the GOP are different from "real Americans"; that they are "people who hate"; that they are "up at six in the morning trying to figure out which minority group they're going to screw today"; and that in the upcoming presidential campaign, they "are going to fight...smear...lie...and hate."* – Source national review online, July 28, 2004. This is real hateful stuff, which hardly furthers meaningful debate on how to resolve the serious issues of our day.

There's a part of me that wants to give democrats the benefit of the doubt and believe that they are mostly thoughtful people that I just have a difference of opinions with on many (ok most) issues. However when they associate with left-wing nuts like Moore my faith in today's democrat fades. I find it hard to believe that elected democrats truly embrace the garbage that Moore spews. Don't get me wrong, I'm not saying Michael Moore should be censored. Liberals censor free speech, not conservatives. However, if liberals want to be thought of as serious people instead of shrill extremists, they need to stop embracing the Michael Moore types of the world. I also hope that it's just an urban legend that elected Democrats in Washington have weekly conference calls with members of MoveOn.org. Here's a little hint for Harry Reid, you are not going to get salient ideas from that crowd. They certainly are not going to be the types of ideas that would be embraced by grassroots Americans.

Conservatives Need Not Apply

I also find it interesting that when either Michael Moore or Charlie Sheen produces a leftist anti-American movie, the liberals cheer them as courageous forces that are at the height of their profession. On the other hand the Hollywood leftists all but crucified Mel Gibson for producing the movie 'The Passion of the Christ'. How dare a famous actor make a movie that showed a level of respect towards the Christian religion! Remember, to the Hollywood left, conservative views held by many Jews and Christians are at the core at what is wrong in the world today. When Gibson produced the movie, many said that his career was over, and that the movie would be a box office flop. The movie was a huge box office success.

There are a couple of lessons that can be learned from this. First of all, it is leftists that threaten people that don't agree with their views. They are the ones that practice intimidation and censorship. You don't hear conservatives in Hollywood stating that the careers of either Michael Moore or Charlie Sheen will be ruined by producing the crap that they do. Secondly, well produced movies that are respectful to Christians can make money. Hey liberals, conservatives go to the movies and buy popcorn too. The big Hollywood decision makers that refused to financially support Gibson's project missed out on this huge box office bonanza. They let their financial decisions be driven by their extreme liberal bias, and it cost them millions of dollars.

The Dixie Chicks alienated a lot of their fans with their anti-American stance. I found it interesting that when their careers started to tank, they cried censorship. The Dixie Chicks are to dimwitted to realize that only the government can censor speech. They hurt their own careers by offending their fans, who are not all anti-American airheads. In fact, a lot of people that listen to country music are quite patriotic. These ditsy Dixie Chicks aren't smart enough to know the difference between government censorship and free market forces. Of course, to a liberal they're all geniuses and we conservatives are all simpletons.

What I find truly disheartening is that today's Hollywood leftist are so full of hate that they can't even get behind something as positive as Sean Hannity's Freedom Concerts. For the past several years, Sean Hannity has been putting on Freedom Concerts to benefit the children of American military personnel that have died fighting in the war on terror. The money raised is to help send these kids to college. This is truly a beautiful thing that Sean is doing, in the spirit of a Bob Hope type volunteerism. Liberal Hollywood types not only won't participate, they are actually critical of this. How removed from reality do you have to be to actually think that charity concerts to raise money for such a tremendous cause is wrong? I guess liberals can't even find it in their hearts to support the sons and daughters of our brave troops, much less the troops themselves.

9/11 Conspiracy Theories

I find it interesting that on the one hand, liberals always say what a complete idiot President Bush is. At the same time, this supposedly intellectual lightweight was to have masterminded the 9/11 attacks fooling the nation and the entire world. Bush and Cheney have been accused by the loony left of having carried out the 9/11 terrorist attacks so they could conduct military operations in the middle-east because as well all know the war is about the oil. If that were true, where are all the lucrative oil contracts? Why hasn't Bush taken over the Iraqi oil fields? Gas prices should be around $1/gallon if the liberal blood for oil theory was correct.

Noted expert on metallurgy Rosie O'Donnell said that the collapse of the Twin Towers had to be an inside some since steel beams don't melt. Huh? Where does she think steel beams come from? Do they grow out of the ground in the precise shape and dimensions needed to construct steel buildings? The obvious truth is that this is just another instance of Rosie making a complete ass of herself and letting her anti-American ignorance shine for the entire world to see.

Charlie Sheen is producing a movie called "Loose Change" which states that our government was behind the 9/11 attacks. Fahrenheit 9/11, the movie by Michael Moore was another bunch of liberal dribble. Moore's anti-American film is credited with receiving the longest standing ovation at the Cannes Film Festival in 2004. OK – this is the same France that was violating the United Nation's sanctions against Iraq by regularly doing business with Saddam. Perhaps France's reason for not supporting the ouster of Saddam is because they were doing business with him in violation of United Nations sanctions. Here's another news flash - a lot of the French are a bunch of snotty elitists.

I vacationed in France back in early 2001. Yes, I know but we all make mistakes. While I did meet some very nice people there, I have never been treated so rudely in my life. As an American, I was denied service in restaurants, and some taxies refused to take me as well. That's fine I just won't make the same mistake again, and visit France. I won't soil that country with either my presence or my money ever again. Let enough Americans stop vacationing in France, and we'll hurt them right in the wallet. Again, free market forces at work. This is the same France that didn't have the testicular fortitude to defend their own country from the Nazi onslaught. Those guys sure loved Americans in 1944 – 45 when we freed them from the horrors of German occupation. During my last day in France, I found myself in a bar having a couple of beers with some other American tourists. We all agreed that if Germany ever attacked France again, they could keep it. Another lesson for the left, Americans liberate, we don't conquer. The United States has freed more people from tyranny than any nation in the history of the world. No country in the history of mankind has used it great military might with such restraint. All people alive today that can breath the air of freedom owe a level of thanks to the American soldier.

America, a country that promotes the arts showers Hollywood types with fame and wealth beyond belief. Where else could a dimwitted blonde get paid more than most of us make in a year to appear on Larry King Live shortly after being released from jail? Poor Larry had to speak slowly and use small words. These are the same people that complain about America at every turn. How long would Rosie survive living in Iran if she spoke out against its Government? For that matter, how wealthy and famous would any of these Hollywood types be in Iran or Syria? The last time that I checked, North Korea doesn't have a huge Hollywood-type industry making a bunch of people wealthy beyond belief.

Bill Cosby

I didn't want to leave the chapter about Hollywood types without mentioning a truly powerful force for good. I've got to say that I just have the utmost respect for Bill Cosby. While far too many black celebrities are promoting a destructive lifestyle, Mr. Cosby is bucking that trend. He dares to go out to the black community and say that many of the social ills that plague them are in fact self inflicted. Issues such as dropping out of school, unwed mothers, drug use and violence are destroying the black community. He urges blacks to take responsibility for their actions and work to improve their own lives. Now, that is a positive message as opposed the usual garbage that you hear in Rap music from people such as Akon. It's unfortunate that there are more black celebrities promoting the kind of crap that Akon does, as opposed to what Bill Cosby is preaching. Keep it up Bill you're helping far more people in the black community than any liberal government program ever will.

Chapter #3

Illegal Immigration

Conservatives are pro-immigration. We all realize that the vast majority of us are descendants of immigrants. However, we came here legally, obeying the laws of the land. While most of us still hold a level of pride in the country that our ancestors came from, we consider ourselves Americans. Immigrants bring their diversity culture and ideas that adds to the fabric of our society, the great melting pot that is America. Growing up in the north east, there is a huge mixture of Americans that immigrated from various countries. We came here to become Americans, not to change the country to what we had just left. We fly the American flag, and not the flag of the country we immigrated from.

As I am writing this chapter, the shameful amnesty bill has recently been defeated in the Senate. It is also worth noting that the title of this chapter is 'Illegal Immigration'. Of all the attacks that liberals hurl at conservatives, the ones used surrounding this particular issue are truly shameless. Conservatives are not anti-Hispanic nor are we anti-immigrant. We do however get angry when people enter into this country illegally, violating our laws and showing a gross lack of respect for our Nation's sovereignty.

Enforcement First

A lot of Americans have lost faith in our government to have the will to do what's right for **We the people**. In a post 9/11 world, many of us find it stunning that our government can't find it within itself to enforce our borders. Protecting the citizenry is the single most solemn duty that our elected officials have. Terrorists are using the same unguarded border crossing as the illegals are. Yet, according to noted military expert Ted Kennedy, fighting illegal immigration is akin to chasing landscapers. This is not a man that takes enforcing our nation's immigration laws seriously.

Our southern border is being overrun by human smugglers and drug runners. Violent attacks against our border patrol agents are becoming a daily occurrence. Why not, our government is encouraging this type of violence. Border patrol agents Ignacio Ramos and Jose Compean are both behind bars facing more than 10 years in prison for shooting a Mexican drug smuggler who had crossed into this country illegally with 700 pounds of drugs. I guess he works as a landscaper part-time hey Teddy. After being shot, the drug smuggler self-deported himself back to Mexico. Since it was dark, and the suspect fled, Ramos and Compean didn't know if he was in fact shot or not. It was a representative of our own government that went to Mexico to speak to the drug smuggler and convince him to file charges against Ramos and Compean. In exchange for agreeing to testify against the border patrol agents, this drug smuggling scum bag was given legal status enabling him to cross into the United States anytime he wants. I wonder if as an American citizen I would get this type of understanding treatment if I were caught with 700 pounds of drugs. Here's even a better question. What would the Mexican government do to me if I tried to cross into their country with 700 pounds of drugs and shot at their border patrol agents? I urge President Bush to pardon both Ramos and Compean. Performing your duties as a border patrol agent shouldn't expose you to a 10-year prison sentence. Liberals will state that we can't use our troops to enforce the border because it would be a violation of Posse Comitatus, which states that U.S. troops can't be used for law enforcement. There's a difference between protecting our borders, and using soldiers as local police to enforce traffic laws.

A year after a law was passed to build a fence on the border between the United States and Mexico, less than 100 miles has been completed. Considering that the length of our southern border with Mexico is nearly 2,000 miles long, at this rate it will take some time to complete the work. The Director of the U.S. Border Patrol David Aguilar said in May of 2007 that it would take until 2013 to attain operational control of the U.S./Mexico border. We're at war with terrorists that want to destroy us, we have illegals flooding into this country in unprecedented numbers, and our country can't dedicate the necessary resources to build a fence any sooner than 2013. The Secretary of Homeland Security Michael Chertoff could release the $4.4 Billion of monies that have been allocated to address illegal immigration to jump start getting the fence built. The Secretary of Homeland Security should start protecting the homeland. You think the President and Congress have low approval ratings now, wait until we're attacked by terrorist that are in this country illegally. If Mrs. Bill Clinton is elected in 2008 – heaven help us – there will be absolutely no effort to stem illegal immigration. Quite the opposite this woman will likely legalize all 12 + million illegals right away by executive order. Remember, she's a woman of vision, and there are the 2010 and 2012 elections to consider.

Liberals will put water stations in southern Arizona to help make crossing the summer desert safer for illegals. Now, at a human level, I don't want to see anybody die in the hot Arizona desert. However, should we really be aiding those that are coming into our country illegally? Perhaps instead of water stations, how about picking up the illegals and giving them some water while they're being deported.

Mexico's Hypocrisy

Mexico has been very critical of the debate in this country about the illegal immigrant issue. Like our own loony lefties, they accuse such actions as being purely racist. Of course, when one takes a look at Mexico's immigration laws, one would have to conclude that they are down right draconian. **Legal** immigrants into Mexico can not run for elected office, can not hold a government job, and are not eligible for social services. Only immigrants that are skilled professionals are allowed into Mexico. With all of their landscapers here in the United States, you'd think they'd have a shortage over there. Here's another thing, the immigration quota in Mexico is around 3,000 per year. That's the legal quota. Try to cross into Mexico illegally, and see how open and welcoming that country will be.

Don't expect to get any kind of support at all from the government of Mexico in stopping the flow of illegals into our country. On the contrary, they hand out informational pamphlets instructing their citizens on how to cross into the United States illegally. Mexico even has a resort that holds mock illegal border crossing as a form of entertainment. There are so many hidden tunnels between the United States and Mexico used by drug smugglers, that it puts those of the fabled Stalag 13 and Hogan Heroes to shame. They have absolutely no respect for our sovereignty. Mexico has a direct financial interest here. They allow millions of their unskilled citizenry to illegally enter into the United States. It is estimated that these illegals send billions of dollars back to Mexico each year to support their families. This is found money for the Mexican economy. In fact, Mexico's second biggest source of revenue is the money their illegals send back from the United States. Mexico is a dirt poor oil rich nation. Now there's a concept that you wouldn't normally think would go together. More accurately, Mexico has an incredibly corrupt government that has no real interest in working to address the poverty that ravages the nation. They'd rather export their problems to the United States.

Most Illegals are Law Abiding People

One of the arguments that the left repeatedly makes is that most illegals are law abiding people. For the record, what percentage of people that have crossed into this country illegally have broken the law? The obvious answer is all of them – 100%. The act of coming into this country illegally is in and of itself a crime. The majority of them also commit the felony crime of perjury. For tax purposes, we all sign a W4 form when we are hired on to a new job. So when an illegal provides a fake social security number, and signs the W4, they've committed two more crimes. They've committed perjury by signing the form knowing that the information they've provided is inaccurate. They have also provided fake, often forged documents. Many also commit the crime of identity theft. The social security numbers that they are using belongs to somebody. Oddly enough, Arizona leads the nation in identity theft.

Try traveling down to the southern part of the American border. Thanks to the illegals, a state of chaos and lawlessness has pretty much taken over. They trespass onto the lands of American citizens that live there. The citizens are faced with a no win proposition. They can't rely on the federal government to protect them. If they try to take matters into their own hands and defend their homes, they risk winding up in prison like Ramos and Compean. Many are reduced to locking themselves inside of their homes as illegals trespass on their properties and trash them. Interesting how if Americans would litter and trash the country side, the environmentalist would be having a fit demanding that strong legal action be taken. However, since those that are trashing the place happen to be illegals, it's ok.

It's estimated that 25% of the prison population in this country is comprised of illegal immigrants. We could potentially reduce our prison population by a quarter if we aggressively enforced our immigration laws. A few of years ago in Arizona, a couple of coyotes had a shoot out on the highways. For those of you who don't know, coyote is the term used for those engaged in the disgusting act of human smuggling. Here I thought that liberals were against human smuggling. I wish they'd clarify their position on that issue. Coyotes are truly a ruthless bunch who stuff people into vans, into the hollowed out bodies of automobiles and other sub-human conditions. They think nothing of leaving people to die in the desert. The only thing these coyotes care about is the money that the illegals pay them to smuggle them into the country. If the American military really did treat Al-Qaeda prisoners like coyotes treated their own brethren that would be a disgrace.

Ted Kennedy's History on Immigration Reform

The fact that Ted Kennedy is on the wrong side of this, or any, issue shouldn't come as a shock to anybody that's to the right of Rosie O'Donnell. What I do find somewhat stunning, is that this man has a 42 year history of being repeatedly wrong on this issue. Securing our borders, stemming the flow of illegals coming into this country, and what to do with those who are already here is by no means a new problem. In 1965, it was the Hart-Celler immigration reform bill that was signed into law by Lyndon Johnson. In defense of this bill, on February 10, 1965, Kennedy who at the time was the chairman of the Senate immigration subcommittee, stated that *"our cities will not be flooded with a million immigrants annually ...the present level of immigration remains substantially the same...and...(the bill) will not inundate America with immigrants from any one country or area."* In 1986, the Massachusetts Senior Senator came out in support of the Simpon-Massoli immigration reform bill. Here ole' Teddy stated that *"This amnesty will give citizenship to only 1.1 to 1.3 million illegal aliens. We will secure the border henceforth. We will never again bring another amnesty bill like this."* Flash forward to 2007, where Kennedy now states that *"Now it is time for action. 2007 is the year we must fix our broken border system."*

The truth of course is that the number of people from Mexico coming into our country illegally has exploded over the last 20 years. This is not only an increase in raw numbers, but an increasingly higher percentage of Mexican nationals are choosing the illegal route over legal immigration. In the late 1980's, less than 30% of Mexicans coming into this country did so illegally. Flash forward to 2007, a whopping 85% of people coming into this country from Mexico are doing so illegally. We are being inundated with illegals. In 2000, the Center for Immigration Studies report to Congress that the Simpon-Massoli bill had in fact given amnesty to 2.7 illegals, more than double the 1.1 – 1.3 million that Kennedy reported at the time. So, as our elected leaders are saying that there are approximately 12 million illegals in this country, in reality that number could be closer to 20 – 25 million. Left unchecked, and right now it is unchecked, by 2030 we could have well over 50 million illegal aliens in this country. Areas of the country such as Arizona and southern California are beginning to lose their identity now. Double or triple the amount of illegals, and the American citizen will be in the minority in the southwest.

Our in the beltway politicians are so detached from the rest of the country that they were surprised by the national outrage over this latest bill. The senior Senator from Arizona John McCain co-sponsored this farce of a bill with Senator Kennedy. Coincidentally, at the same time Senator McCain was also seeking the Republican Presidential nomination. There is nothing and I mean nothing on a domestic level that will kill your presidential aspirations as a republican faster than co-sponsoring this bill. Between this and McCain's shameful finance reform bill that he co-sponsored with Senator Russ Feingold, he should admit he's a democrat and change his party affiliation.

We Can't Deport 12 Million Illegals

A common argument of the left is that we can't possibly locate and deport the estimated 12 million Mexicans that are in this country illegally. For one thing, I don't buy that issue. I bet if 12 million Americans decided to stop paying taxes that the Internal Revenue Service would find us in no time flat. When the illegals have the nerve to march in protest demanding the right to break our laws at will, I'm sure that ICE could find some deportees quite easily.

Beyond that, there are several things that our government could do to 'entice' the illegals to leave on their own accord. First off, fine companies that regularly employ illegals. If the fines are steep enough, companies will stop hiring them. Better yet suspend, and in more egregious cases revoke, the operating licenses of businesses that hire illegals. In fairness, the government should create a verification system that would enable companies to check on the authenticity of the documents that a potential new-hire produces.

Cut off federal funding to cities or states that refuse to prosecute crimes committed by illegals. This would be an effective deterrent to municipalities that refuse to perform their legal duties.

I'm both stunned and outraged when I hear of an illegal killing people while driving drunk. I'm not only outraged by the loss of life, but the fact that in most cases, the illegal had been arrested numerous times for drunk driving and other crimes in the past, yet was allowed to stay in the country. If you are arrested for a crime and are in this country illegally, you should be deported - period. That's after you've served out your sentence. No illegal should be allowed out on bail while awaiting trial for a crime. Here's another news flash for the left, illegals are flight risks. I'm not talking about going back to Mexico, but fading into the shadows. You know that place where our government can't find them.

Illegals convicted of felony crimes in the United States should also be denied the opportunity to ever legally come into this country for life. Think about it, you've come into this country illegally, and then have committed other felony crimes. Why would we want to allow you to legally come in? There are plenty of law abiding people waiting in line trying to come into this country legally. They are the ones that will enrich us as a nation.

Another argument of the left is that we can't deport illegals because it would break up their families. Here's a question for the left, if as an American citizen I am sent to prison for a crime isn't my family broken up too? Another thing, nothing stops the deported illegal from bringing the rest of their family back with them. When you break the law you assume certain risks. When you involve your families, you expose them to such risks as well.

Require proof of citizenship or legal residency to receive any social services. At the risk of sounding harsh, I don't want my tax dollars going give government handouts to illegals. In Arizona, they have a grocery store chain called Food City, which caters to Latinos. Most Food City grocery stores also have services that allow you to wire money. You can stand back and watch illegals wire cash back to Mexico, and proceed to purchase their groceries with food stamps. Stop giving illegals government hand outs. We can not afford to be the free meal ticket for illegals. The government should also put a dollar limit on the amount of money that can be wired to Mexico. The inability to send money back to their families in Mexico would be another effective deterrent.

Publicly funded education should be reserved for people that are in this country legally. Proof of legal status should be required for entry into a public school and university. Amazingly, many public universities grant illegals in-state tuition if they've lived in the state long enough to meet residency guidelines. Think about that for a moment. If as an American citizen, your child lived in New Mexico all of their life, and wanted to go to school in Arizona, you'd have to pay out-of-state tuition. If an illegal, who had been evading the authorities long enough to avoid deportation applies to the same university, they get in-state tuition. American citizens pay higher tuitions costs to government funded public universities than illegals do. We are rewarding illegal behavior. Our government is paying people who break our laws. They are giving illegals benefits denied to American citizens.

Stop the anchor baby syndrome. The 14th amendment to the Constitution was not intended to give citizenship to the offspring of those that are in this country illegally. For one thing the amendment states that, *"All persons born or naturalized in the United States, and subject to the jurisdiction thereof, are citizens of the United States and of the State wherein they reside."* When the amendment was written, we didn't have an illegal immigrant problem. It was never intended to give de facto citizenship to the offspring of illegals. Our elected officials know this, and also know that this mis-interpretation can be changed without further amending the Constitution itself. Simple legislation would suffice, and would also make a huge difference for the better in this area.

The American Economy is Dependent on Illegals

This argument is so ludicrous I find it hard to believe that liberals will say it with a straight face. The strongest economy on the planet is dependent on 12 million people, the vast majority of whom don't have a high school education. The left will say that without illegals, our crops would rot in the field. Then again, a bogus argument. The United States already has a high yearly quota for both legal immigration and seasonal (temporary) workers. With the right numbers, we'd have plenty of workers to perform these types of jobs.

In fairness, it is true that our economy has developed a certain amount of dependency on the work performed by illegals. That doesn't mean that we shouldn't enforce our immigration laws. Would democrats make the same argument if instead of illegals in 2007, the issue was black slaves in 1860? Consider the impact on the economy of the south that freeing the slaves would have! Come to think of it, democrats did make the same argument 147 years ago. Doing the jobs that legal/free Americans won't do. At least liberals are consistent.

As far as illegals performing the work that we won't, I find that insulting as well. I'm certainly not afraid of hard work, and in my youth worked as a landscape laborer and in fast food. The reason that many such jobs are monopolized by illegals is the language barrier they introduce. It's pathetic, but many Americans can't get a job working for a fast food restaurant in states like Arizona. It's because the language of the kitchen is Spanish. How do fast food restaurants in the northeast operate? Do they come to Arizona and California and bus illegals across the country to work in their restaurants? Illegals take jobs away from lower income Americans. These are the same people that the democrats are supposed to care about the most. Now, a handful of illegals planning on attacking Fort Dix. The liberals have got me there. Attacking a United States military installation is a job that Americans just won't do.

Our country has room for one flag and one language. I'm paraphrasing statements made by President Teddy Roosevelt back in 1907. If Teddy had made those statements today the left would have his image removed from Mount Rushmore. Illegals don't come here to become Americans and add to the fabric of our society. They come here refusing to speak English, demanding we change to meet their needs. Immigrants living in the northeast came from countries that speak over a dozen different languages. Oddly enough, you don't see government employees having to speak German, Italian, French, Greek, Portuguese, etc. America is known as the great melting pot. As legal immigrants we all add to the richness of society with what we bring from our 'mother' country while at the same time becoming Americans. Illegals have no desire to become Americans or to learn English neither do they have an allegiance to the United

States.

It's estimated that for every dollar that an illegal pays in taxes, they use up $3 in government services. That's education, fire, police, prisons, roads, welfare, etc. If the 12 million illegals were to leave the country tomorrow, the government would find itself saving billions of dollars every year. The influx of illegals to California is so bad, that they can't build schools fast enough to keep up with the growth.

Many illegals use hospital emergency rooms as their primary care doctors. Skinned knees and other serious boo boos flood emergency rooms. By federal law hospitals can't refuse to treat anybody. Many hospitals in southwestern states have been forced to close their emergency rooms to avoid bankruptcy. At the risk of sounding cold blooded, I don't want my tax dollars going for free health care for illegals. In fact, beyond a one-way trip back to Mexico, I really don't want to give illegals one dime of my hard earned dollars.

Now, in all fairness there is a group of Americans that does get free health care. Do you know what group it is? Come on now remember this is a book about the insanity of liberalism. OK – another group besides illegal aliens that gets government paid health care is criminals. Yep, if you're in prison you get tax payer funded healthcare. Now, I'm not suggesting that prisoners should be neglected, but at the same time, should a death row inmate be put at the head of the line to be given a kidney transplant? I'd rather see the kidney go to somebody that isn't on death row.

A New Liberal Voting Block

The reality is that is actually a huge power grab on the behalf of democrats who are looking for millions of new voters. These people will not vote republican, so the right has nothing to gain and everything to lose. They will hasten the down fall of Social Security, Medicare and other 'entitlement' programs. These programs will either have to be dramatically changed, or tax rates will have to be raised significantly to make up for the extra costs. When I say changed, I mean that benefits to everybody, legal and illegal will have to be greatly reduced. Liberals are so anxious to secure their new voting block that they are willing to forgive any back taxes owed by illegals. Ask yourself, how many American citizens would the IRS let get away with not paying taxes for 10 years or even 5 years. We'd face back taxes, along with huge fines and penalties. Yet, as part of the 2007 bill, our government was planning on forgiving any back taxes owed by illegals.

The Border Crossed Us

Many illegals will state that they didn't cross the border, the border crossed them. The meaning being that much of the southwestern United States was once part of Mexico hence they have every legal right to be here. So, let's look at the merits of that position for a moment. For one thing, we're not talking about people that have lived in the same houses for generations since before the United States took over those lands as a result being the victor of the Mexican War of 1846 – 1848. This was in the wake Texas succeeding from Mexico in

1845 and becoming part of the United States. 'Remember the Alamo' was an American battle cry at that time. The majority of the people making this argument have illegally crossed into our sovereign country within the last 20 years long after that war was over. These people demonstrate a total lack of respect for any rule of law by stating such a ludicrous position.

Secondly, for right or wrong, much of the lands of the earth that are controlled by one nation today belonged to a different nation at some time in its history. The hard truth is that countries throughout time have battled over territory. As a general rule, it is the victors that get to take land from the conquered. It we were to lend credibility to their argument, the largest country on the planet would be England. In their history, England had conquered so much land that at one time it was said that the sun never sat on the British Empire. So, if liberals truly buy into the illegals' argument that we illegally stole their land from them, then countries like India have some real explaining to do to the British monarchy.

A Pathway to Citizenship

There is one thing that I totally agree with the left on. Individuals that are in this country illegally, that are hard working people should have a path to legal status. The truth is that there already is a path to legalization for them. They can go back to Mexico, and migrate legally into this country. Being in this country illegally shouldn't put you on a fast track to legal status ahead of those trying to follow the rules. It's why so many Americans were against the 2007 immigration bill. Z visas, Y visas and other kinds of non-sense. Illegals today can go back to Mexico and apply for legal immigration into the United States. That's without paying a fine. Most Americans also had no faith that our government would enforce many of the provisions of the bill. We have laws against illegal immigration now that aren't being enforced, what good would a new law do?

The left is also wrong when they say that illegals want a path to citizenship. The majority of illegals don't want to become American citizens. They want our freedoms, access to our welfare and schools etcetera, while most have no desire to join the American experience. If they did, they would learn English and stop flying the Mexican flag. The following is an exchange between a news reporter in Houston and a protestor marching in for the rights of illegal immigrants.

Houston Texas - May 1, 2006.

Jim Moore reporting for a Houston TV station:

Jim: Juan, I see that you and thousands of other protesters are marching in the streets to demonstrate for your cause. Exactly what is your cause and what do you expect to accomplish by this protest?

Juan: We want our rights. We will show you how powerful we are. We will bring Houston to its knees!

Jim: What rights?

Juan: Our right to live here...legally. Our right to get all the benefits you get.

Jim: When did you come to the United States?

Juan: Six years ago. I crossed over the border at night with seven other friends.

Jim: Why did you come?

Juan: For work. I can earn as much in a month as I could in a year in Mexico. Besides, I get free health care, our Mexican children can go to school free, if I lose my job I will get Welfare, and someday I will have the Social Security. Nothing like that in Mexico!

Jim: Did you feel badly about breaking our immigration laws when you came?

Juan: No! Why should I feel bad? I have a right to be here. I have a right to amnesty. I paid lots of money for my Social Security and Green Cards!

Jim: How did you acquire those documents?

Juan: From a guy in Dallas. He charged me a lot of money too.

Jim: Did you know that those documents were forged?

Juan: It is of no matter. I have a right to be here and work.

Jim: What is the "right" you speak of?

Juan: The right of all Aliens. It is found in your Constitution. Read it!

Jim: I have read it, but I do not remember it saying anything about rights for Aliens.

Juan: It is in that part where it says that all men have Alien rights, like the right to pursue happiness. I wasn't happy in Mexico, so I came here.

Jim: I think you are referring to the Declaration of Independence and that document speaks to unalienable rights .. Not Alien rights.

Juan: Whatever.

Jim: Since you are demanding to become an American citizen, why then are you carrying a Mexican Flag?

Juan: Because I am Mexican.

Jim: But you said you want to be given amnesty ... to become a US citizen.

Juan: No. This is not what we want. This is our country, a part of Mexico that you Gringos stole from us. We want it returned to its rightful owner.

Jim: Juan, you are standing in Texas. After wining the war with Mexico, Texas became a Republic, and later Texans voted to join the USA. It was not stolen from Mexico.

Juan: That is a Gringo lie. Texas was stolen. So was California, New Mexico and Arizona. It is just like all the other stuff you Gringos steal, like oil and babies. You are a country of thieves.

Jim: Babies? You think we steal babies?

Juan: Sure. Like from Korea and Vietnam and China. I see them all over the place. You let all these foreigners in, but try to keep us Mexicans out. How is this fair?

Jim: So, you really don't want to become an American citizen then.

Juan: I just want my rights! Everyone has a right to live, work, and speak their native language wherever and whenever they please. That's another thing we demand. All signs and official documents should be in Spanish. Teachers must teach in Spanish. Soon, more people here in Houston will speak Spanish than English. It is our right!

Jim: If I were to cross over the border into Mexico without proper documentation, what rights would I have there?

Juan: None. You would probably go to jail, but that's different.

Jim: How is it different? You said everyone has the right to live wherever they please.

Juan: You Gringos are a bunch of land grabbing thieves. Now you want Mexico too? Mexico has its rights. You Gringos have no rights in Mexico. Why would you want to go there anyway? There is no free medical service, schools, or welfare there for foreigners such as you. You cannot even own land in my country. Stay in the country of your birth.

Jim: I can see that there is no way that we can agree on this issue. Thank you for your comments.

Juan: Viva Mexico!

Juan was certainly not alone in his views as they were likely shared by a large portion of the illegals participating in the march. This is not a case of people wanting to become part of the American experience. They want to get all the benefits that our country has to offer without any intention of becoming Americans. If illegals are truly outraged by injustice, they should fight for the injustices in Mexico. They should fight the corruption in their own country and work to change things for the better. Instead, they've given up on their own country, and have no intention of weaving themselves into the rich fabric of America.

Illegal Immigration and the War on Terror

The left has argued that there is no correlation between illegal immigration and the war on terror. Several of the individuals that were planning to attack Fort Dix were here illegally. Many of the 9/11 hijackers were living in this country on expired visas. While most illegals that cross over our southern border are Mexican, Arab terrorists are exploiting the unguarded crossing as well. It is truly stunning that our government doesn't see the national security interest in protecting our borders in a time of war.

In addition to controlling illegal immigration, our government should also temporarily stop all immigration from Arab nations. That includes all forms of immigration including both work visas and student visas. While this might seem somewhat harsh, and would impact some law abiding Arabs, it is a protective measure that our government should take. Several of the 9/11 hijackers were in the United States on expired visas. After the attacks in England, do we even want to assume the risk of allowing professionals from Arab countries to come into the United States? Is it in our country's best interest to allow students from Arab countries to study nuclear engineering and other highly technical skills so they can take that knowledge back to the Arab world? If we were to stop all immigration from Arab countries, it would send a strong message how the terrorists are impacting the rest of the Arab community. It is highly doubtful that our country would suffer from a lack of immigration from Arab nations. I believe that we would be able to find enough American citizens to drive taxis and work as convenience store clerks. While this is certainly not a politically correct stance to take, it is one that is in our country's best interest.

Chapter #4

Indoctrination

(Liberal Control of Education and the Media)

What liberals fear most of all is the free flow of information. Whether it's educating our young in the school system, or what we can be exposed to on television and the radio, liberals want to control it all. One of the most solemn duties we as adults have is to provide the best education that we can for our children. It's not only what is best for them, it's also what is best for our country. Education is the best way out of poverty, it's how diseases are cured and generally raises us up as a species. Most of the inventions that came out of the 20th century were made right here in the good ole' USA. This is not a matter of snobbery insinuating that Americans are better than everybody else. It speaks to the power of freedom and the importance of education.

Education not Indoctrination

To liberals, education is not to enlighten but to indoctrinate. For example, you can't teach creation in public schools because of course it would lend one to believe in God. So liberals insist on teaching Darwin's theory of evolution, which fits into their godless agenda. Never mind that a hard look at both theories favors creation over evolution. Even teaching both, and letting students decide for themselves which is more believable would be a more honest educational approach. Remember, for liberals the schools are not a place to educate our young, but to indoctrinate. Liberals will argue that they don't want creation taught in the public schools because it has proven to be false. While there is still debate, creationism has not been debunked in fact it is Darwin's theories that start to crumble under the light of hard scientific scrutiny.

This is the same liberalism that will teach that there is a gene that causes homosexuality in humans. So of course, being homosexual is a completely natural alternative lifestyle. People don't choose to be homosexual, God makes them that way. Now, this is not a point to start bashing gays and lesbians, but to illustrate how liberals are indoctrinating our young in the public schools with their loony agenda. I do wish liberals would get their story straight on this. Homosexuality can't be a product of evolution since lesbians and gays can't procreate which is bad for the continuation of the species. Are liberals saying that God made people homosexual? I thought that liberals didn't believe in either God or creationism? Do you see how liberalism falls apart under scrutiny.

There are actually professors in this country that have forced students to watch Al Gore's fantasy movie "An Inconvenient Truth". What would the ACLU do if a college professor made Sean Hannity's book 'Let Freedom Ring' required reading? The 'fairness doctrine' is strictly to silence conservative talk radio. It sure as hell is not to ensure that both sides of an issue are fully and openly discussed. If it was, the universities around the country would have to hire a whole bunch of conservative professors. Try to get hired in as a university professor and be even slightly to the right of Sean Penn. While discussed more deeply a subsequent chapter, a liberal's idea of affirmative actions is conservatives need not apply. Its one thing for professors to talk about politically charged topics in a political science class. Today, there are university professors spewing their anti-American nonsense in all types of classes ranging from English to Chemistry. These people should be working for Air America, and not being paid a salary at a tax payer funded university.

Sex – Drugs & Rock n' Roll

I think one of my favorite examples was at an assembly at Boulder Valley School that was teaching children about sex and drugs. During their 90-minute 1960's era hippie love fest school officials weren't teaching abstinence or to stay away from drugs, but rather encouraging both sex and illegal drug use. Pre-marital sex and illegal drug use are interesting things to be promoting in the public schools. They were also promoting all types of sexual activity including; men on men, women on women as well as men on women. Well, at least heterosexuality hasn't been banned yet. This was a mandatory assembly for students in a public school that promoted illegal drug use and all types of sexual activity.

While many students were stunned and parents outraged, to liberals it was conservative troublemakers like Bill O'Reilly that stirred up trouble. They don't see that perhaps as parents we want to cover those rather personal subjects with our kids, and not government bureaucrats. Perhaps we have different ideas about drug use and sexuality that we want to impart on our children. Of course, since these incredibly inappropriate topics had a liberal bias, the ACLU remained silent. What would the ACLU have done if the school had talked about the virtues of abstaining from pre-marital sex, and how having abortions often causes serious depression issues in women? How about instead of illegal drug use, the school was advocating cigarette smoking. Now that would have had the whole lot of them fired. Liberal mindset – cocaine good – tobacco bad.

So, let's recap here for a moment. No God in school, homosexuality is completely normal and natural, and pre-marital sex and illegal drug use amongst teens is expected.

Freedom of Choice

You want to drive a liberal off the deep end, mention that you favor school vouchers. The voucher system would introduce competition into the field of education. Standards would rise and everybody would benefit. I find it interesting that liberals will attack monopolies on almost every front except in education. Students that attend private schools, religious school and even those that are home schooled regularly beat out their public school counter parts in educational assessments. Both as an American, and as a parent, I want the best education for our children. That's what I care about, and not protecting the monopoly of the public school system.

Many companies state that they are sending work overseas because the United States is not producing enough highly skilled graduates. I'd say that the liberal monopoly over education is less than totally successful. That is if their goal is to provide the best quality education for our children. This, as a conservative, is exactly what I believe it should be.

The last time that I checked, the Kennedy children didn't attend public schools. Here liberals are supposed to be the champions of the poor, yet with their policies, only those that can afford the tuition can send their children to private schools. How different would our country be if politicians were forced to send their own children to public schools, thus having to live with a failed system that they impose on the rest of the country? They'd probably pass a school voucher system in a matter of days.

Vouchers that are good in any school would empower parents with the freedom of choice to send their children to any school that wanted to. When I say any school that doesn't exclude the public schools. It simply means that public schools should have to compete with other educational institutions. Competition always gives we the consumers a better product at a lower price. Liberals always state that if we only spent more on education, we'd be able to solve all of the problems. Some of the worst school districts in that nation spend the most money on a per student basis. In Washington D.C., they spend over $10,000/year per student, and the district is one of the worst in the country. For that kind of money, the kids should be taught by full professors, and have Emeril Lagasse preparing their lunches. It's not that we don't spend enough money on education it is the ineffectiveness of a government controlled monopoly that is the problem.

Liberals will also state that government vouchers can't be used to send children to religious schools because of the Constitutional separation of church and state. For one thing, the Constitution does not have a clause demanding the separation of church and state. Secondly, the state would not be mandating that children be sent to a given religious school. It would be the parents choosing to send their children there. There again, parental choice and freedom of religion, which by the way is in our Constitution.

The two most positive things that our government could do today to improve the quality of education for our children would be to pass a voucher system, and to eliminate the U.S. Department of Education. That bloated bureaucracy doesn't help any children get a better education, or put more money into the classroom. It's just another monument to government ineffectiveness. Cut it out altogether and use that money to cover part of the cost of the voucher program.

Liberal Fear Effective Education

Liberals do not want a truly effective education system that promotes excellence and an open and honest exchange of ideas. In fact, the last thing that liberals want is a well educated electorate. Liberals want big government, and need multi-generational welfare recipients to maintain their voting base. Giving people access to effective education is a huge threat to democrats. Well educated people that work hard and pay taxes are generally more conservative than uneducated people who live off of the government.

The most dangerous thing to a liberal is an open arena of ideas. It's why they want to control education. It's also why conservative talk radio and the Fox News Channel are both hated by the left. Millions listen and watch as appropriate, as they shine the light on the liberal hypocrisy. They're so mad that they are looking to destroy conservative news outlets by passing a 'fairness doctrine'. Never mind that we have government paid liberal radio (NPR). To a liberal, if you can't beat them - demonize and destroy them.

Air America, liberals' attempt at talk radio on the open market was a flop. It didn't fail because of censorship or because of Rush Limbaugh and Sean Hannity, it failed because it couldn't compete. To a left-wing democrat, most of the country shares their liberal ideology. That being the case, Air America should have been a huge success. I guess Al Franken isn't as in touch with the rest of the country as he claims. During a particular showing of Hannity & Colmes, Alan Colmes stated that the reason his radio talk show only had a listening audience of roughly one million, a small fraction compared to Sean's, was because his show wasn't on prime-time. Hey Alan, ever think that the reason your radio show is on late is because of its small audience and not vice-versus. Perhaps the only program you can compete with is Coast to Coast with Art Bell. I will say in fairness to Alan that he is against the actions of Hugo Chavez and his shutting down a Venezuelan television station for airing views not shared by the dictator. I do want my book to be somewhat fair and balanced.

Conservative talk radio is generally entertaining, informative and thought provoking, while liberal talk radio is negative and shrill. I really can't see listening 'three hours a day every day' to a talk show host saying how much America sucks. Conservative talk radio is also more open and honest about the hot topics of the day. They don't parrot a party line. They will be critical of President Bush or an idea the Republicans are supporting if they feel they're on the wrong side of the issue. President Bush was in full support of the 2007 Immigration bill.

Conservative talk radio opposed it, in direct opposition of the President and many prominent Republicans. It's that level of intellectual honesty and probative thought that many find so attractive about conservative talk radio.

Roughly 90 percent of people in the media identify themselves as being liberal. Conservative talk radio and the Fox News Channel are dominating the airways not because they outnumber the media types in sheer volume, but because they offer a better product. Liberals want to control what we learn and what we hear. Information is power, and they want to control all information that is imparted to us.

Of course, liberals not being able to control what we the people hear is a huge threat to them. They miss the gold old days when we all got our news from Walter Cronkite. Right before the 2004 Presidential election Dan Rather produced documents damaging to George W. Bush. These documents, supposedly created back in the early 1970's were actually produced on a 21st century computer. This obvious attempted fraud on the American people is just another example of liberals wanting to control what we are hear. It's also a stark reminder of their total lack of ethics and honesty. The hard truth is that the liberal's 'fairness doctrine' is on par with Hugo Chavez shutting down a television station in Venezuela that was critical of his policies. Is that where liberals have gone to in this country? What's next, Nazi-style book burnings?

I don't expect the dinosaur media to all of a sudden sound like Sean Hannity or Laura Ingram. However, intellectual honesty for goodness sake would be a nice change. When the 'news' is obviously nothing more than an extension of the democrat party, no wonder people turn them off. Media executives watch their audiences diminish their profits fade, and refuse to face the reality that they need to deliver an honest product.

Here our founding fathers considered a free press so critical that it's in the 1st amendment. Their idea was that a free press would serve as a guard against the government from becoming too overbearing and trying to control the information we the people had access to. A free press would also be an honest critic of the government, calling our elected officials to task and demanding that they explain their positions to the electorate. Sounds like Thomas Jefferson wouldn't be supportive of the 'fairness doctrine'.

Liberals complain that talk radio has become too powerful, and was responsible for the demise of the 2007 immigration bill. Bill Clinton owes his Presidency to an extremely leftist press. While in office, he regularly committed acts of perjury, witness tampering, suborned perjury, and other illegal acts while getting a free pass from the press. Hell, he even bombed an aspirin factory in the Sudan to take attention aware from the Lewinsky affair. While some liberals like to claim he did nothing wrong, his acts were so bad, Arkansas disbarred him. The press couldn't even bring themselves to state that a married man in his late 40's having sex with an intern half his age in the Oval office was wrong. Where was the National Organization of Women decrying how wrong it is for a male boss to illicit sex from a young female subordinate? You don't even want to know what that pervert asked Monica to do with his cigars. Had Ronald Reagan done this, the press would have been all over him. If it wasn't for what has been called *'presidue'*, Clinton's semen on Monica's dress, he would have stood by his lie to the nation. Nixon was not involved in the burglary at the Watergate hotel. He was involved in the cover up, and a President that lies to the American people about an illegal act should be removed from office. At least that's what a young Mrs. Clinton thought back then. She actively supported Nixon's removal from office. It's funny how opinions change from the 1970's to the 1990's and when the liar is your own husband.

This is who the liberals consider the smartest women in the world. The same person who was certain that the accusations against her husband about having an affair with Monica was part of a 'vast right-wing conspiracy'. The same woman that while testifying before congress about Whitewater used the phrase "I don't recall" some 50 times. The same woman that magically found documents in the upstairs personal residence of the White House two years after they had been subpoenaed. That is why the investigations into White Water and the Rose Law firm didn't end in any convictions. Only organized crime is as skilled as the Clinton machine in thwarting investigations. This is same woman whose socialist healthcare plan was so extreme that it was even too far out for her own party. If she weren't married to Bill she would be nothing more than a crooked attorney screwing people over in Arkansas.

I've often asked liberals what they think if Laura Bush would run for President in 2008. The obvious answer is that they believe being a first lady does not qualify you to run for the presidency. So let me get this straight. A first lady from Arkansas that moved to New York just before running for an open Senate seat in that state is qualified to run for President but not Laura Bush. I do find liberal logic hard to follow.

You'd think that the NOW crowd would be more supportive of strong successful women that made it on their own merits, and not on their husband's coat tails. NOW should be touting the achievements of women like Condoleezza Rice and not Mrs. Bill Clinton. I guess NOW isn't interested in a truly brilliant woman who has reached the pinnacle of power on her own, and women of color to boot. The truth of it all is that NOW is not for women's rights, but for liberal rights. Conservatives need no apply.

Chapter 5

Taxation

One would like to believe that by definition, taxation is a means to bring monies into the government treasury to enable it to perform their appropriate functions. Now, there are of course spirited debates concerning what people believe the appropriate functions of the government are. This is particularly true of the federal government. If only they would concentrate on; providing for the national defense, regulating interstate commerce and coining money. The duties actually outlined in the Constitution. The government doesn't even print our paper money anymore they've outsourced that to the Federal Reserve. They sure as hell perform an entire slew of other functions not specifically delegated to it by the Constitution. That's an entire other discussion altogether. I will say that if only our elected officials in Washington D.C. would read the 10th amendment again. With regards to taxation, the hard truth is that for liberals, tax policy is not a means to fund government, but rather to coerce certain types of behavior, and to create class envy and class warfare.

Tax Cuts for the Rich

Whenever the subject of lowering taxes is mentioned, liberals will always decry how it is nothing more than tax cuts for the rich. I find it interesting that across the board tax cuts supposedly only benefit the wealthy. Across the board tax cuts will be more money back in the hands of all taxpayers. It is true however that tax cuts across the board will put more money back in the hands of rich people than poor people. This is because of the simple fact that the wealthy bear the greatest portion of the overall tax burden. According to the Congressional Budget Office, the top1% of wage earners in this country pay roughly 38% of the entire tax burden. The top 20% of wage earners pay approximately 80% of the entire tax burden. The bottoms 50% of wage earners pay around 5% of the tax burden. The rich are not getting a free ride, quite the opposite they are getting royally screwed.

The present day tax scale can't be considered to go from 0 – 100, with the poorest people not paying any taxes at all. The scale should be more like -20 – 100, since if you don't work at all, liberals will pay you. In San Francisco, the city will pay you to be homeless. As a result, homeless people from around the nation flock to San Francisco for the free handout. That's money for cigarettes, booze, drugs whatever the homeless want to spend it on. The city has no expectation that any of the homeless will use the money to try and lift themselves out of their current situation. Liberals have turned welfare from a hand up to a hammock. Damming somebody to a life of homelessness is what liberals consider compassion.

Taxes and Big Business

Another favorite complaint for liberals is that corporations don't pay their fair share of taxes. I personally wouldn't care if corporations didn't pay any taxes at all. Corporations are not tax payers, they are tax collectors. They pass on the cost of the taxes that they are forced to pay on to us, the consumer, by building it into the prices of their products or services.

Liberals also love to decry the evils of Big Oil and Big Tobacco, as why tax cuts for businesses are bad. Well guess what, big government makes far more money in taxes from the sale of a gallon of gasoline than big oil does. In some instances, they make 5 – 10 as much depending on the particular state and their taxes. In some states as much as 60 cents per gallon is nothing but a combination of state and federal taxes. The local station actually selling the gas makes less than 10 cents per gallon on average. It costs our 'friends' in the middle-east between $1 - $2/barrel to remove the oil from the ground. Then they turn around and charge us $60/barrel. If it really was expensive to take the oil out of the ground, I doubt the price of a gallon of gas in Riyadh, Saudi Arabia would be as low as $0.91/gallon. They also don't have to deal with the various seasonal blends and additives as oil companies have to here in the United States. With all of this, I don't hear liberals screaming about Arab price gauging.

Likewise, our government also makes far more money from the sale of a pack of cigarettes then evil big tobacco does. Arizona, Maine, Michigan, and Washington all collect $2.00 or more in taxes on the sale of a pack of cigarettes. New Jersey has the highest tax rate collecting $2.57 in taxes on the sale of a single pack of cigarettes. If people suddenly stopped smoking tomorrow, our government would loose more money than big tobacco. This is because the tobacco companies would still be able to benefit from the sale of cigarettes to other countries. Don't be fooled for a second with the government's claim that the tobacco tax is to pay for the medical care of the people that get sick from smoking. The tax collected goes into a general fund, and is no more set aside to cover the medical expenses of smokers as the federal government has a Social Security lockbox.

Now, personally I am no fan of cigarette smoking. I don't smoke, and I discourage my children from smoking also. However, we live in a supposedly free society where people are allowed to make their own decisions. If the government truly believes that smoking is that dangerous then they should ban it outright. As it stands right now, our government is making a killing (no pun intended) on the sale of a product they deem of extreme danger to our health. Kind of like a drug dealer only there's more money involved.

It's not a Zero Sum Game

Liberals will tell you that we can't cut taxes because we need to pay for their particular pet program of the day. Most recently, they decry the cost of the war on terror as to why the Bush tax cuts must be allowed to expire. This of course amounts to a de facto tax increase. However, every time government has cut taxes, revenues into the government have increased. It happened in the 1960's under President John Kennedy who was by no means a right wing Republican. It also happened under Ronald Reagan in the 1980's and most recently with President George W. Bush. In fact, in the wake of the Clinton/Gore recession, and the attacks on 9/11 the Bush tax cuts are the main reason why the economy was able to recover so quickly. The stock market has more than doubled since its post 9/11 lows. This was not by accident, but was largely due to President Bush cutting taxes in combination with lower interest rates. A country trying to tax itself into prosperity is like standing in a bucket and trying to lift yourself up by its handle. In other words, a country can not tax itself into prosperity. The best way to spur on a struggling economy is to put money back into the private sector by lowering taxes.

Liberals often point to the dramatic raise in deficits during the Reagan years and blame his tax cuts. The truth is that under Reagan, monies to the treasury almost doubled as a results of his tax cuts. The deficits were a result of the government spending more than even the Reagan windfall brought in.

Class Warfare

To a liberal, taxation is not a mechanism to get monies into the government coffers, but to punish achievement and create class warfare. Look at the economic devastation that Jimmy Carter caused by his punitive tax policies. They included; high unemployment, double digit interest rates and high inflation. The term for the Carter economy was stagflation. This is yet another legacy of that man's failed presidency. When President Reagan lowered tax rates across the board, the economy grew at an unprecedented pace. You know, I often wonder when I hear Alan Colmes state that we can't cut taxes and pay for the war on terror at the same time, how he hasn't learned anything from sitting next to Sean Hannity for more than 10 years. On the one hand, I want to believe Alan is an intelligent and honest guy. On the other hand, one of those two assumptions has to be false if he truly believes that tax cuts mean lower revenues into the government treasury. The evidence to the contrary is all around us.

Simplify Our Tax Code

The tax code in the United States is so large and so complex that it is almost beyond the realm of human comprehension. It is also riddled with loop holes for special interest groups that bribe – I mean donate to – politicians in exchange for favorable actions in this area. It's stunning that as a nation we spend billions on attorneys, accountants and tax preparers trying to make any kind of sense of the tax code. How many people dread April 15th? I know one thing, if elections were moved from early November to early April, there would be real action taken to fix this entire mess.

Both a flat tax and a national sales tax have been tossed around by conservatives as possible alternatives to the system that we have today. Both ideas would allow the government to do away with the Internal Revenue Service, arguably not the most beloved government bureaucracy.

A flat tax would both simplify paying taxes, and result in a more equitable distribution of the tax burden on all Americans. It doesn't make sense that wealthier Americans should pay a higher percentage of their income to the government. As a nation we need to reward achievement and not punish it. Remember, poor people don't start businesses and hire workers, wealthy people do. Now, if limousine liberals feel guilty for not paying their fair share of taxes, nothing is stopping them from paying more. They can write checks to the government any time they want to.

Having a national sales tax is also an interesting idea. Since it's based on consumption, those that buy more would pay more. I could also see exempting certain food staples as a way to ease the burden on lower income Americans. Yes – conservatives are compassionate. I would be concerned about the government adopting a national sales tax without first repealing the 16th amendment. The concern is that they'd bring back the income tax, while leaving the national sales tax in place. As a short history lesson, it was the 16th amendment to the Constitution that gave the government the authority to lay and collect income taxes from *we the people*. Can you believe that prior to 1913, taxes on income were deemed unconstitutional. Hard to believe today that our government functioned for over 130 years without an income tax.

At Least Allow Us to Die Tax Free

Just about everything we do or buy is taxed in one way or another. When you work, your wages are taxed. If you take that money and invest it, any monies that you make are also taxed (capital gains). Currently, if you take a loss on the sale of a stock, your maximum annual tax deduction is $3,000. So, if you make $50,000 on the sale of a stock, you're taxed on the entire amount. However, if you loose $50,000 you can only deduct $3,000. Is it just me, or is that crazy. You can't even die in this country without the government taxing you. How many families have lost their farms because they couldn't pay the inheritance tax on the death of a parent?

Tax Freedom Day for 2007 in The United States was April 30th. This is according to the Tax Foundation, which is a Washington, D.C. based tax research organization. That means that on the average we all spent the first four months of 2007 working to pay our taxes, and only have eight months of our annual wages to support both ourselves and our families. That's 25% of our labors going to the government. How big of a raise did you get last year? For most of us it was far less than 10%. If the government were to cut taxes by 1/5, it would amount to a pay increase of 5% to the American worker. Personally, I'd like that very much. For most people, their tax burden is a greater expense than their mortgage payment, car loans, healthcare costs – anything. Paying taxes shouldn't be the single biggest expense Americans face everyday.

The advent of people buying goods on-line is a real problem for our government. The government doesn't like it because in most cases, we get to purchase items without paying any sales tax. In most cases, the shipping charges are lower than what the sales tax would be. There have been grumblings about trying to put a government tax on anything purchased on-line. These guys are truly insatiable. I wonder if the liberals are chastising Al Gore for creating this huge tax loophole.

Stop Spending So Much

It's not that we're under taxed, it's that the government over spends. When is the last time spending for a government program was reduced. I don't mean a reduction in the amount of growth in spending of a government program, but an actually reduction from the previous year's levels. With the exception of Carter and Clinton eviscerating our military and putting our country in danger, the answer is never. Dare mention reducing the growth of a government program other than national defense, and liberals start shouting how children will die and the elderly will starve. If Teddy Kennedy had his way, the government would still be subsidizing the horse n' buggy industry.

To be intellectually honest, I will say that as a conservative, I am disappointed in President Bush and the Republican led congress. They had six years to reduce spending, having a majority in the legislative branch, and a Republican in the White House. The unfortunate truth is that spending was not cut in fact President Bush didn't veto any spending bills during that six year period. There are a couple of lessons to be learned here. When Republicans are in the majority they need to act like it. Republicans loose elections when they don't govern like conservatives, a la 2006.

Republicans are afraid that people won't believe that they are truly conservatives, while democrats fear people won't believe they're really aren't liberals. One of the major issues that Bill Clinton campaigned on in 1992 was that he was going to give the middle-class a tax cut. Once in office, Mister Honesty himself in reality proceeded to pass the largest peace time tax increase in this Nation's history. There's another Clinton running for the presidency now. She's not to be trusted either.

Politicians spend billions of dollars each year on pet projects for their states. Earmarks, as they are called, are nothing more than attaching garbage spending onto bills that have nothing to do with the particular piece of legislation itself. Since the president doesn't have a line item veto, they can't cut the pork away from the substance of the particular piece of legislation that Congress sends up for him to sign. It's all or nothing. Former member of the Klu Klux Klan,

Senator Robert Byrd has brought in so much pork into West Virginia it is truly stunning. There are many roads, schools, hospitals, etc. that bear his name in tribute for him having his snout deep into the government trough. Apparently fleecing the tax payers of the other 49 states helps those that vote for Byrd see beyond his KKK roots.

I find it interesting that elected officials were so outraged by the financial shenanigans of Enron. Now, don't get me wrong, I'm not defending what Enron did. However, there's not a private sector business on the face of the planet that can waste money on the scale that our elected officials do. Ken Lay was a two-bit pick-pocket compared to the type of government graft and waste our elected officials practice. Ken Lay didn't have $90,000 dollars stuffed in his freezer. Lay screwed up by not knowing that you have to be an elected official, ideally a liberal, to play around with money that freely.

You think Enron's books were bad, true auditing the books of either the Senate or the House. Many a non-profit charitable organization has been fined for not spending enough of the dollars that they raise on the cause that they are supporting. Guess which entity wastes more money prior to passing it on to the poor. You got it – our own government.

Our government is also the single largest employer in the world. Even excluding military personnel, they still have the single largest payroll on the planet. During tough times, private sector companies look for ways to reduce expenses. Ever known our government to cut spending during economic slow downs. Democrats have removed themselves for any semblance of fiscal responsibility and ignore any kind of economy forces. They spend at will.

Luxury Taxes on the Working Class

Liberals love to tax high dollar luxury items. Since most Americans can't afford to buy yachts and other high dollar luxury items, it's an easy sell for them. Of course, when the rich stop buying these high dollar luxury items because of the extra costs of the higher taxes, the working class gets hurt also. The working class Joe that looses his job building yachts because of the luxury tax, is being hurt more than the wealthy having to sail their used boats for a couple of more years. Of course, industries that supply the raw materials used to build the new yachts are impacted as well. Suffice to say, the reach, and hence the pain, caused by such a tax goes far beyond their intended victims.

The same holds true for taxes on hotel rooms and car rentals. Politicians will say how the money is only from out-of-state visitors, and it doesn't affect the locals. Of course, money spent on taxes for both hotel rooms and rental cars is money that doesn't find its way into local shops and restaurants. The local economy is impacted, as travelers have limited resources and monies spent on taxes are not being spent on local goods and services. Here again, an open dialogue about the impact of tourism taxes would be refreshing. I have no respect for politicians that lie to the electorate.

Chapter #6

Religion:
(The Liberal Assault on Judaism and Christianity)

I think that one of the things that bothers me the most about liberalism is the near total lack of intellectual honesty. Another glaring example of this is their argument against both Judaism and Christianity. Liberals will state that our Constitution guarantees a separation of church and state. The first amendment says no such thing. This is not the opinion of a right-wing religious zealot, as I am sure the left will label me, it is the actual text of the amendment itself. With regards to religion, the first amendment reads as follows: "... *Congress shall make no law respecting an establishment of religion, or prohibiting the free exercise thereof;"* In plain English, congress can't pass a law establishing a government religion. No politician have ever suggested establishing *The Church of the United States*, and liberals know it. The first amendment also states that congress can't prohibit the free exercise of religion. So, when liberals ban school prayer, demand the cancellation of Christmas plays and stop our children from singing Christmas carols they are in fact violating the first amendment.

Judeo-Christian Roots

As any school-age child knows, our country was founded by people searching for among other things - religious freedom. Freedom to pray any way that they choose, including opting not to pray at all. The country was not founded as a religious free zone as liberals would have us believe. References to God can be seen throughout our founding documents. For example, below is an excerpt from The Declaration of Independence.

"When in the Course of human events, it becomes necessary for one people to dissolve the political bands which have connected them with another, and to assume among the powers of the earth, the separate and equal station to which the Laws of Nature and of **Nature's God** *entitle them, a decent respect to the opinions of mankind requires that they should declare the causes which impel them to the separation. We hold these truths to be self-evident, that all men are created equal, that they are* **endowed by their Creator** *with certain unalienable Rights, that among these are Life, Liberty and the pursuit of Happiness."*

Many of our presidents have invoked the name of the Almighty in speeches they have delivered to the Nation. The following is an excerpt from George Washington's first inaugural speech that he delivered on April 30, 1789.

"Such being the impressions under which I have, in obedience to the public summons, repaired to the present station; it would be peculiarly improper to omit in this first official Act, my fervent supplications to that **Almighty Being who rules over the Universe, who presides in the Councils of Nations, and whose providential aids can supply every human defect, that his benediction may consecrate to the liberties and happiness of the People of the United States"**

I wonder what today's liberals think of Washington's speech? It would be far more informative to hear what Washington would say about today's liberals attack on our freedom of religion.

President Franklin Roosevelt delivered the following speech to the Nation

on June 6, 1944 (D-Day)

"My Fellow Americans: Last night, when I spoke with you about the fall of Rome, I knew

at that moment that troops of the United States and our Allies were crossing the Channel

in another and greater operation. It has come to pass with success thus far. And so, in

this poignant hour, **I ask you to join with me in prayer: Almighty God:** *Our sons, pride*

of our nation, this day have set upon a mighty endeavor, a struggle to preserve our

Republic, our religion, and our civilization, and to set free a suffering humanity. Lead

them straight and true; give strength to their arms, stoutness to their hearts, steadfastness

in their faith. **They will need Thy blessings.** *Their road will be long and hard. For the*

enemy is strong. He may hurl back our forces. Success may not come with rushing speed,

but we shall return again and again; **and we know that by Thy grace,** *and by the*

righteousness of our cause, our sons will triumph. They will be sore tried, by night and by

day, without rest -- until the victory is won. The darkness will be rent by noise and flame.

Men's souls will be shaken with the violences of war. For these men are lately drawn

from the ways of peace. They fight not for the lust of conquest. They fight to end conquest.

They fight to liberate. They fight to let justice arise, and tolerance and goodwill among *all Thy people. They yearn but for the end of battle, for their return to the haven of home. Some will never return. **Embrace these, Father, and receive them, Thy heroic servants, into Thy kingdom.** And for us at home -- fathers, mothers, children, wives, sisters, and brothers of brave men overseas, whose thoughts and prayers are ever with them -- **help us, Almighty God,** to rededicate ourselves in renewed faith in Thee in this hour of great sacrifice. Many people have urged that **I call the nation into a single day of special prayer.** But because the road is long and the desire is great, **I ask that our people devote themselves in a continuance of prayer.** As we rise to each new day, and again when each day is spent, **let words of prayer be on our lips, invoking Thy help to our efforts.** Give us strength, too -- strength in our daily tasks, to redouble the contributions we make in the physical and the material support of our armed forces. And let our hearts be stout, to wait out the long travail, to bear sorrows that may come, to impart our courage unto our sons wheresoever they may be. **And, O Lord, give us faith. Give us faith in Thee;** faith in our sons; faith in each other; faith in our united crusade. Let not the keeness of our spirit ever be dulled. Let not the impacts of temporary events, of temporal matters of but fleeting moment -- let not these deter us in our unconquerable purpose. **With Thy blessing, we shall prevail over the unholy forces of our enemy.** Help us to conquer the apostles of greed and racial arrogances. Lead us to the saving of our country, and with our sister nations into a world unity that will spell a sure peace -- a peace invulnerable to the schemings of unworthy men. And a peace that will let all of men live in freedom, reaping the just rewards of their honest toil. '*

*Thy will be done, **Almighty God.***

Amen.

By the standards of today's left-wing radicals, Franklin Roosevelt would be considered a Christian conservative. His speech would have been condemned, and he probably would have been attacked by organizations such as MoveOn.org and the ACLU.

Religion versus Relativism

When liberals claim that there is no place for prayer, religious speech, references to God or to religious symbols by government officials or in our public buildings, it is simply not true. It is also both insulting and intellectually dishonest to place the belief of no God (atheism) above Judeo-Christian beliefs. Their religious belief of an absence of an almighty should not be allowed to trump the over 90% of Americans that do believe in God. Law suits that have been brought up attempting to remove any semblance of religion are generally initiated by liberal extremists and atheists. Simply put, Jews don't complain about Christmas carols, and Christians generally aren't offended by a Chanukah song.

The truth of the matter is that it is liberals that are uneasy with much of the preaching of Judeo-Christian religions because they teach a level of morality. Liberalism is all about what feels good, with no such thing as right and wrong. The North American Man Boy Love Association (NAMBLA) is an organization that promotes older men having sex with underage boys. In straight talk, that's dirty old men molesting children. Such an organization would certainly have a challenge getting their message to jive with the teachings of either Judaism or Christianity. Of course, the left's courageous leader Nancy Pelosi will gladly march with a member of NAMBLA at a gay rights parade in California. It's a shame she can't find it in her heart to promote the messages of Judeo-Christian values above those of an organization that promotes child molestation.

Of course to speak out in the slightest way against gays, lesbians or even NAMBLA, would have the left label you as a homophobe extremist. I'm not advocating that any government actions be taken against gays or lesbians. I just don't want their lifestyle forced down my throat. OK – perhaps that wasn't the best metaphor that I could have used, but I think you get my point. Sexuality, and opinions of what is proper behavior between consenting adults to a large extent is a personal matter. I don't want liberals telling me that if I personally don't embrace homosexuality that I'm the wacko. Since when has a monogamous sexual relationship between a man and a woman that are married to each other become an extremist right wing conservative value?

If you look at many of the worst dictators throughout history, they all shared a number of traits. One of them surrounded their dictatorial stance on religion. Rather than embrace Judeo-Christian beliefs, such evil leaders usually denied the existence of God, attested to being a god themselves, or as is the case with Islamic extremists, pervert the true teachings of God. Serious power grabs and acting in a way that puts you above all kinds of accountability by definition means that you can't place yourself under God. The governments of Hitler, Stalin and Mussolini were not big on freedom of religion. Hitler would have found it somewhat difficult to say the least to justify his attempted genocide of all Jews had he also promoted Christian values. The bible is not keen on forcing women and children gas chambers.

Christmakah

Something that I do find offensive is the liberal attempt to lessen the importance of both Christmas and Chanukah by trying to combine the two holidays and call it Christmakah. The only similarities between the two holidays is that they are celebrated at around the same time of the year. The similarities stop there. When liberals say that they are alike, and should be combined, it shows a lack of understanding and certainly a lack or respect for both Judaism and Christianity. Of course this is the same form of liberal nonsense that was behind the creation of Kawanzaa. Created by in 1966 by Ron Karenga, to as he put it *"... give a Black alternative to the existing holiday and give Blacks an opportunity to celebrate themselves and history, rather than simply imitate the practice of the dominant society."*

Now, I personally don't have anything against any culture taking pride in the unique qualities of their heritage. Kawanzaa as a peaceful celebration for black Americans is something to be embraced. However, I am offended when it is elevated to the level of a religious holiday. Kawanzaa was created by a 60's liberal that apparently had a problem with what he considered religion for whites, while Christmas and Chanukah both have biblical origins. It would be like elevating NASCAR to the level of a religion. There's a Jeff Foxworthy joke in there somewhere. For the record however, neither Judaism nor Christianity are for whites only. In fact, the skin color of many Israelis is generally more Mediterranean. I'm sure many Christians, would take offense in Karenga's assertion that Christianity is a white religion. I guess he hasn't been to a Baptist church in a while either.

Not All Religions are Banned

Perhaps one of the most telling aspects of the liberal's attack on religion is its selective nature. Any and all references to either Judaism or Christianity are fair game for assaults from the left. However, the religion of Islam is ok. In fact, the University of Michigan-Dearborn recently had foot baths installed. As part of their religion, the Muslim students are required to wash their feet several times a day. The university spent an estimated $100,000 of taxpayer money installing these foot baths to further the religious practice of these Muslim students. Now, I am not necessarily against making accommodations in this manner. However, in the name of intellectual honesty where is the ACLU threatening to bring suit against the University for violating the renowned Constitutional separation of church and state? How would liberals respond if instead of Muslim foot baths, the university had installed Holy Water facets for Catholics?

In 2003, Alabama Chief Justice Roy Moore was targeted by liberals and removed from office for defying a federal court order demanding the removal of a Ten Commandments monument from the rotunda of the Alabama Supreme Court building. So to be clear on where liberals stand on religious displays, Muslim foot baths are ok, but the Ten Commandments are not. I can certainly understand how Bill Clinton would take issue with things such as the seventh commandment which states *"Thou shalt not commit adultery"* and the ninth, *"Thou shalt not bear false witness"*. Clinton's affair with Monica while he was in office was the subject of a widely circulated joke stating that the eleventh commandment read *"Thou shalt not show they rod to they staff."* Conservatives are just more upbeat and funnier than liberals are.

No Religion in Schools

There is no prayer allowed in public schools, that's unless you're a Muslim of course. Some schools opted to let students observe a moment of silence. They could use it for prayer if they chose, or for some private contemplation. Liberals fought that too, as even a moment of silence was too close to recognition of religion for them. Liberals have attacked religious references at the start of sporting events and students have been assailed for daring to make any kind of reference to God during their graduation speeches. During the horrors at both Columbine and Virginia Tech I can guarantee you there was prayer in school. I also dare any member of the ACLU to try and bring suit against any of the students or teachers for praying in school as they were forced to live through those horrible events.

Liberals won't allow creationism to be taught in schools because to believe in the theory of creation is to believe in God. Never mind that Darwin's evolutional monkey theories have been debunked over time. The truth is not what is important. Never mind that we haven't found any half-monkey / half-human creatures walking around. The total lack of intermediary species is not what is important. To a liberal, Darwinism must be true or else you'd be forced to believe in an all powerful God that created life on this planet. We can't have any of that.

I wonder how long it will be until religious programs on television will carry warnings for 'adult content'. People praying on camera will be deemed more offensive than any kind of illegal drug use or promiscuous sex. Liberals already want have movies and televisions shows that have people smoking cigarettes to carry more restrictive ratings. So I guess 'The Andy Griffith Show' and 'It's a Wonderful Life' will carry adult ratings. I suppose shows like South Park are ok just as long as Cartman doesn't light up. Just as long as there's no cigarette smoking involved. I wonder what liberals would think about the characters if they starting smoking a crack pipe or enjoying a hit from a marijuana bong?

Of the many definitions of religion one reads that it is *'a specific fundamental set of beliefs and practices generally agreed upon by a number of persons or sects:'* Liberal's devotion to the beliefs that they hold is a kind of religion to them. If you doubt me, try having an honest intellectual debate with most liberals on any number of topics that they deem as absolute truths and watch their reactions. Try debating the merits of man-made global warming with Al Gore. Just don't schedule the meeting with Al in the winter you don't want to risk getting stuck in a blizzard.

Chapter #7

Global Warming:

Global Warming - the religion of the extreme left. There have been left wing politicians and limousine liberals decrying how the world will end as a result of the ravages of global warming that we humans are causing. Purchasing carbon offsets, and living carbon neutral is the recent craze, and is a way for these left wing extremists to maintain their extravagant lift styles while being able to have clear conscience. Make not mistake, this is not a hard science. This is yet another attempt by the left to control our lives and increase the power of government.

Man Made Global Cooling

The left can't even make up its mind whether we're supposed to be causing global warming or global cooling. As recently as the 1970's, the Earth was supposedly in danger of a second ice age as a result of our effects on the climate. The big scare back then was that our aerosol cans were harming the environment and causing global cooling. A 1971 paper in the journal of *Science* theorized that the effects particulate pollution such as smog could block the sun light and cause global cooling. It was estimated that the mean surface temperature of the Earth could decrease by as much as 3.5 C. If sustained over a period of several years, such a reduction could trigger an ice age. So, smog caused by driving our cars can cause global cooling.

Did noted climatologist Al Gore review the results of that study before they were made public? Remember, that Al Gore has stated that the single gravest threat to the world today is the automobile. In order to stop the imminent destruction of the planet from global warming, we must all stop driving immediately. I'd like to see Al Gore stop using cars and private jets, and travel solely either by horse n' buggy on land or by sail boats over the water.

In the early 1970's, The National Science Board, the governing body of the Nation Science Foundation stated that; *During the last 20 to 30 years, world temperature has fallen, irregularly at first but more sharply over the last decade. Judging from the record of the past interglacial ages, the present time of high temperatures should be drawing to an end . . . leading into the next glacial age.* In 1975, The National Academy of Science had a slightly different take. *The climates of the earth have always been changing, and they will doubtless continue to do so in the future. How large these future changes will be, and where and how rapidly they will occur, we do not know..* There was even the term called nuclear winter. An ice age caused by things such as volcanic eruptions (not man made), and oil fires. Noted environmentalist and humanitarian Saddam Hussein set fire to the Kuwaiti oil fields as he retreated during Operation Desert Storm. I don't recall a massive nuclear winter resulting from his actions.

The Junk Science of Global Warming

To the left, the issue of man made global warming has already been settled. It is a cold hard fact that is not open to any kind of further discussion or debate. Never mind that many of the assertions that Al Gore made in his movie

'An Inconvenient Truth' have been debunked by science. This is both before and after he made this ludicrous movie. Al Gore claims that Himalayan glaciers are shrinking and global warming is to blame. Yet the September 2006 issue of the *American Meteorological Society's Journal of Climate* reported that, *"Glaciers are growing in the Himalayan Mountains, confounding global warming alarmists who recently claimed the glaciers were shrinking and that global warming was to blame."* Gore has also claimed that global warming is the cause of increased tornado activity. Yet, the United Nations Intergovernmental Panel on Climate Change stated recently that there has been no scientific link established between global warming and tornadoes. Now, the United Nations can be called a lot of things, but a right wing organization is certainly not one of them.

Al Gore also claims that the snowcap atop of Africa's Mt. Kilimanjaro is shrinking and that global warming is to blame. Yet according to the November 23, 2003, issue of Nature magazine, *"Although it's tempting to blame the ice loss on global warming, researchers think that deforestation of the mountain's foothills is the more likely culprit. Without the forests' humidity, previously moisture-laden winds blew dry. No longer replenished with water, the ice is evaporating in the strong equatorial sunshine."* Another claim by our most esteemed climatologist is that global warming is causing an expansion of the African deserts. However, in the September 16, 2002 issue of *New Scientists* it was reported that, *"Africa's deserts are in 'spectacular' retreat . . . making farming viable again in what were some of the most arid parts of Africa."* Al Gore has also claimed that the Antarctic ice sheet is melting because of global warming. Yet the Jan. 14, 2002, issue of Nature magazine reported Antarctica as a whole has been dramatically cooling for

decades. More recently, scientists reported in the September 2006 issue of the

British journal Philosophical Transactions of the Royal Society Series A:

Mathematical, Physical, and Engineering Sciences, that satellite measurements

of the Antarctic ice sheet showed significant growth between 1992 and 2003.

And the U.N. Climate Change panel reported in February 2007 that Antarctica is

unlikely to lose any ice mass during the remainder of the century.

The left's claim that the planet is warmer today than in any time in its

history as a result of man made forces is simply not correct. Global temperatures

were actually higher during the middle-ages. Say what you will about the politics

of King Arthur and the Knights of the Round Table, but I can guarantee you those

guys were not driving around in automobiles, or burning fossil fuels in any way

shape or form. England is not as warm today as it has been in that Nation's

history. Tax records of the past show that grapes used to be grown in the

England. That industry has died because it is not warm enough to grow grapes in

England anymore. What this tells us is that global temperature changes, both

warming and cooling trends are a result of factors other than you and I driving

our car and simply living our lives.

Anthony Watts has uncovered an interesting fact, which can be found on

his web site, www.surfacestations.org. Many of the government's temperature

measuring stations are improperly placed, giving erroneous readings. That's of

course erroneously high readings. Many thermometers were placed close to

airplane runways, barbeque grills and more. These are the ones that they use to track the official temperatures of the United States, and led them to state that 2006 was the hottest year on record.

Global Warming a Stellar Tragedy

There is also evidence of global warming on Mars, Pluto and Jupiter. How are liberals going to blame mankind for that? Should the Martians stop driving their SUVs or turn their AC down? Perhaps there's a market for those small fluorescent light bulbs on Jupiter. Tongue and cheek aside, the phenomena of other planets within our solar system experiencing global warming as well would tend to illustrate that what we are experiencing here on Earth is not caused by man. Al Gore screamed how Bush preyed on our fears, by 'tricking' the nation in to go to war in Iraq. Islamic terrorism is a real man made threat that we can do something to combat. The planet going through a warming cycle is beyond our control. Yet Al is preying on the fears, and gullibility of liberals with his – the sky is falling – warnings.

Carbon Dioxide is Not a Pollutant

Many liberals will also state how we are destroying the Earth by putting so much carbon dioxide into the air. For the record, carbon dioxide is not a pollutant; rather it is a naturally occurring gas. Since plants and trees 'breath' carbon dioxide and in turn give off oxygen, there may be a benefit here. The additional carbon dioxide in the air would be like us living in an oxygen enriched environment. I certainly hope liberals aren't against the prospect of there being more plants and trees. Plants and trees provide shade (that's cooling for you liberals) and produce oxygen, which is also very beneficial. They also provide food and shelter for many species of insects and animals.

Conservation

I'm not suggesting that we shouldn't try and use less coal and oil. In fact, reducing our dependence on foreign oil would benefit this country in many ways. For one thing, it would place a financial drain in the terrorism industry if we stopped buying so much oil from the middle-east. The truth is that through good old American ingenuity, many of the appliances that we use today are far more energy efficient than those of 15 to 30 years ago. A new refrigerator will use far less energy than one built in the 1970's.

Alternative forms of energy such as solar, wind and nuclear power would also reduce our dependency on fossil fuels. You want to see liberals go bananas, suggest building a windmill farm near them. The limousine liberals had a fit when it was suggested to put a windmill farm in Nantucket Sound. Even though it would have supplied most of the energy the area required, looking at a bunch of windmills is for those of us in fly over country, and not the for liberal elites. Ted Kennedy is not going to standby and let the view from his Hyannis Port estate be obscured by a bunch of unsightly windmills. This was a clear example of a 'not in my backyard' (NIMBY). Windmill farms also have the unfortunate habit of acting as bird choppers. You may please the environmental crowd, but PETA isn't going to be happy with you.

Another inconvenient truth for Al Gore and the rest of the global warming crowd is that the methane gas that cows emit has far more of a greenhouse effect on the planet than anything man has come up with. Are we supposed to kill all the cows in the world to stop them from heating up the planet because they fart to much?

If you want to see the one thing that has the greatest impact on the climate of the world, just look up onto the sky. That large yellow thing that we call the sun has far greater of an impact on our climate then my driving my kids to school does. Do liberals really believe that my SUV has a greater impact on the world's climate than either volcanic eruptions and solar flares? I will say that I drive a 4-cylinder Honda CR-V. Since it's not a mammoth SUV, I guess in my own way I am helping.

The city of Denver Colorado has plans to change the world by adopting policies to reduce green house emissions and reduce the effect of global warming. While there is a certain degree of respect that can be afforded to a mindset of think globally - act locally, the actions of Denver aren't going to have any change to the world's climate. It will however have a negative impact on both the residents and businesses within Denver as they are forced to comply with policies that have no other purpose than to satiate the needs of liberal extremists. I wonder how many businesses will have to leave Denver as a result of these new regulations before the loss of tax revenue forces the politicians to change their minds. Liberals might feel good by passing regulations that harm businesses, but if it costs them tax dollars that's where they draw the line. Liberals first allegiance is to collecting the most tax dollars that they can. It's how they grow government and their own power.

Practice What You Preach

Beyond the obvious question of the near total lack of scientific evidence to support the claims of man made global warming is the fact that Al Gore, John Edwards and other ultra-rich limousine liberal types don't even practice what they preach. If the planet were truly so close to being devastated by global warming, then stop building huge mansions and living life styles that only make you some of the worst contributors to global climate change on the planet.

Al Gore has the unmitigated gall to say that he is living carbon neutral because he is purchasing carbon offsets to make up for the fact that his life style uses up over 20 times the amount of energy as the rest of us. Of course, he actually owns a major stake of the company that he is purchasing the carbon offsets from. So, in other words, by paying himself money Al Gore is neutralizing the effects that his own lifestyle is causing on the global climate. Does that mean that if as Americans we just saved more of our money for retirement that global warming would go away as well?

Al Gore's zinc mine was also a huge source of pollution. This guy might speak about protecting the earth, but he is one of the biggest polluters around. It's the same level of hypocrisy that allowed Al Gore to conveniently forget to mention that he grew up on a tobacco farm while decrying the evils of cigarettes. Al Gore preaching to us about the dangers of global warming while living the lifestyle he does is akin to Michael Moore preaching to us on how to live healthy. A man that looks like 'Fat Bastard' from the Austin Powers movies is not coming from a position of credibility when talking about how to live right. Of course, preaching about how good the healthcare system of Cuba is doesn't help his credibility either.

It's also fascinating to see limousine liberals fly to a Live Earth Concert on their private jets to talk about the dangers of global warming. Only the left will actually come up with a gathering of self important liberals producing tons of 'climate altering' carbon emissions to decry the evils of carbon emissions. You truly can't make this stuff up. It does however make for good fodder for the ½ Hour News Hour.

Global Warming and Kyoto

If we were to attempt to follow what the Al Gore types wanted us to, it would devastate the economies of the world. The Kyoto Accords of 1997 were designed to come up with a world wide agreement to reduce the effects of global warming. That agreement was so bad, that our senate voted 95 – 0 against it. Who was the president of the senate back in 1997? Come on – we all know the answer – yep Al Gore. Apparently he couldn't even convince the democrats to vote for that piece of lunacy. Other countries that didn't sign on to the Kyoto treaty include India and China. From a percentage of the world's population standpoint, that alone is enough to put a major dent into any reduction in the reduction of greenhouse gases. China and India also have emerging economies with far less regulations than we have here in the United States. In short, we can expect some serious pollution and greenhouse gas emissions from those two countries. I doubt Denver Colorado will be able to off set those two countries.

Tiny Fluorescence Light Bulbs are the Answer

According to the global warming crowd, if we all replaced the incandescent light bulbs in our homes with miniature fluorescent light bulbs, it would go a long way to saving the planet. Of course, these light bulbs are manufactured in China. This is not a country renowned for its enforcement of any king of environmental regulations on its manufacturing industries. What China is known for is the extensive use child labor and brutal working conditions.

Fluorescent light bulbs also contain mercury. Unlike the unfounded claims of the dangers of man made global warming, having every household in America use light bulbs containing mercury poses a real health risk. Mercury poses a health risk to both animals and human. Exposure to mercury can have negative health effects including damage to the brain, kidney, lungs, and the developing fetus. This is not to mention the issue of having millions of mercury filled fluorescent light bulbs in our landfills. They will of course break, spilling their mercury allowing it to make its way into our ground water. This is not a smart environmental plan.

Where's The Middle Ground

I could actually have placed a where's the middle ground section in all of my chapters. With regards to global warming, nobody is suggesting that we don't take steps to reduce pollution and to use less CO^2 emitting fuels. Unlike liberals however, as a conservative, I actually have tremendous faith in the ingenuity of the American people, as well as the power of the free market. If the government were to offer tax breaks and other monetary incentives for reducing energy use and developing new technologies, the private sector would take it from there. *'In the present crisis, government is not the solution to our problem; government is the problem.'* President Reagan knew those words to be true, and they're just as applicable today. If the government were to do things such as allow new refineries to be built, permit oil drilling in ANWAR, and fund research into alternative fuels, the private sector would do wonders. The sad truth is that our government's energy policies or lack there of, are part of the problem, and not the solution.

Chapter #8

Energy Policy

We have serious problems with our energy policy here in the United States. We are overly dependent on foreign oil, most of which comes from countries that are not our closest allies. Our economy is far too vulnerable to the whims of Arab extremists that like nothing more than to screw over the western nations. Through it all, liberals have done everything in their power to ensure that we don't reach any level of independence from middle-eastern oil.

Domestic Sources of Energy

We have domestic sources of energy in this country that liberals have done everything in their power to see that we don't utilize. In 1996 Clinton issued an executive order creating the 1.7 million-acre Grand Staircase-Escalante National Monument in Utah, rendering the "low sulfur" coal deposit off limits for commercial mining. The move, for all practical purposes, gave Beijing control of the world's only sulfur free coal through its Lippo Group partner. As a reminder, the Lippo Group included notables such as Moctar Riady and John Huang. Huang met with Bill Clinton at the White House 10 times between the dates of June 21 – 27, 1994. Right after that, Webster Hubbell, who was about to be indicted by a federal grand jury, received $100,000 from the Lippo Group. After that, and shortly after the money was given to Hubbell, Huang was given a high level security clearance and the position of Assistant Secretary of the Commerce Department.

While at the Commerce Department, Huang obtained classified materials on trade deals with Indonesia, China, Japan, Korea and the Middle East. Huang also obtained information on U.S. Patriot missile deals with South Korea and mobile artillery for Kuwait. Huang is given a high level position within the government, along with access to classified information that he passes on to China. This is despite the fact that Clinton was warned against giving Huang a high level clearance. The grown-ups in the government knew that this guy couldn't be trusted. During the congressional investigations of Huang, his answer to many of these uncomfortable issues was for him to take the 5th. China gets access to classified documents, Huang gets off, Clinton gets tons of cash, and the American people get screwed. Yet another fine legacy of the presidency of Bill Clinton.

The Arctic National Wildlife Refuge (ANWR) has large deposits of oil. By some estimates it could contains upwards of 10 billion barrels of oil. Democrats pat themselves on the back for blocking all attempts to open even a small area of ANWR to oil exploration. They say that it will ruin the pristine natural beauty of ANWR, and endanger the wildlife that lives there. OK – let's get real, we're not talking about a major tourist attraction here. After all, ANWR is not the Grand Canyon. The fact is that it is so desolate and cold that the only way to get there is by air. Oil exploration would only make a small footprint in ANWR. The reality is that the only humans that would ever see the oil rigs and housing for the workers would be the workers themselves. It is also a lie to state that oil drilling permanently damages the wildlife that lives in the area. Caribou and other wildlife have not been harmed by the Alaskan pipeline. In fact, some animals actually appreciate the warmth that the pipeline gives off.

Thanks to the environmentalist wackos, American companies were stopped from drilling for oil off the shores of Florida. Now, Cuba is drilling for oil there. Does anybody really think that good ole' Fidel is environmentally conscience and uses the latest technologies to protect the ocean? If a spill were to occur, would Cuba clean up the mess to the extent that an American company would? Hint to the left – hell no they wouldn't.

Oil Refineries

The last refinery built in the United States was in Garyville, Louisiana, and it started up in 1976. Do the math, there hasn't been an oil refinery built in this country in over 30 years. It's not because there's not the need, it's because of liberals and their environmental extremism. Companies don't want to put up with all of the obstacles that liberals put in their way in the form of nonsensical regulations. To make matters worse, twice a year as refineries have to shut down and be retooled for the seasonal blends, causing gas prices to go up.

Most of this nation's oil refineries are located in the Gulf Coast. This puts our capacity to refine oil in jeopardy during hurricane season. This does nothing for the environment, and has a huge negative impact on the entire nation.

Common Sense Energy Policy

A common sense energy policy that includes taking advantage of domestic sources of fuel would benefit our country on many levels. Reducing our dependency on foreign oil doesn't have a down side. Does anybody really think that getting less oil from Iran is bad for America? It costs between $1 - $2/barrel to get the oil from the ground. So when middle-eastern governments charge $60/barrel for oil, there are really sticking it to us. American big oil companies are in reality only minor players on the world's oil market. It is the governments of the middle-east (OPEC) that set the world's oil prices.

We should encourage companies to build more efficient cars and appliances. Government should fund research that will find the next generation of energy such as cars that run on hydrogen. How about giving tax breaks to car makers to develop and build cars that run on hydrogen. Match that with government incentives to gas stations that include hydrogen pumping facilities. The same strategy would apply to cars that would run on corn fuel. We can reduce our dependency on middle-eastern oil, and reduce our overall dependency on fossil fuels. However, it takes a realistic energy policy and not one that is just a bunch of posturing for left-wing environmental wackos.

Chapter #9

Arkansan Chutzpah

What truly bothers me the most about the arguments of the left is the lack of intellectual honesty. For the 'average' liberal, I can write a certain amount of this off to their being well meaning but ignorant. After all, liberalism is a feel good emotional based philosophy, while conservatism is an intellectual based philosophy. What gets me mad is when both elected officials and members of the press openly lie to the American people on issue after issue.

Members of the press have a Constitutional obligation to deliver truthful and honest information to we the people. Their freedom to do so is spelled out in the first amendment. Yet, time and again the dinosaur media has opted to ignore the duties given to them by our Founders, preferring to be nothing more than the media arm of the Democrat Party.

'Pardon' of Scooter Libby

On June 2, 2007 President Bush commuted the 30 month jail sentence of former aide to Vice-President Cheney, Lewis 'Scooter' Libby. The reaction of liberals such as Nancy Pelosi and Mrs. Clinton was nothing but typical liberal hypocrisy. They accused President Bush of having no respect for the rule of law, and even damaging our national security since Libby exposed the identity of CIA super-spy Valerie Plaine. The problem with this level of outrage, is that early on in the investigation, it was known that Libby did no out Plaine, that is was in fact Richard Armitage. While the special prosecutor knew this, he spend two years and wasted tax payer dollars until he had a trophy he could hang on his wall, and that was Libby.

Now, to date, Bush had not fully pardoned Libby, who is still facing probation and a fine of $250,000. How quickly Mrs. Bill Clinton has forgotten some of the people that her husband pardoned while he was in the White House. *Appendix 'A'* has a list of the people that Clinton pardoned. You'll notice that on the last day of his presidency, January 20, 2001, Clinton pardoned over 140 people. Several of the people on this list coincidentally made large contributions to the Clinton library. Yes, under the presidency of Bill Clinton it was possible to buy yourself a pardon.

Clinton - Innocent in Liberals' Eyes

On Fox News Channel's Hannity and Colmes, Alan Colmes has often argued that since the Senate failed to vote to remove Clinton from office, that he is in fact innocent of all charges. For one thing, the Constitutional procedures of impeachment and whether or not to remove a President from office are not criminal proceedings. If Clinton had been removed from office, the vote itself would not have subjected him to any subsequent fines or jail time. These are not judicial proceedings, they are legislative ones. The sad truth is the democrats in the Senate didn't vote to remove Clinton from office despite the overwhelming evidence that he did in fact commit the impeachable acts that he was accused of. Clinton's actions were on par with those of President Nixon. In Nixon's case, the Republican's had enough sense of duty and respect for both the rule of law and for us as Americans to urge him to resign. They were not going to defend him in light of his transgressions. If only democrats had a similar sense of duty. Al Gore may have won the 2000 election if he had urged Clinton to resign, or had resigned himself in protest. It would have given him a level of credibility that he lost in his steadfast support of a man that had obviously committed numerous impeachable offenses. A comparison that I like to make to irk liberals is that Clinton is as innocent O.J. Simpson. Simpson wrote a book outlining how he would have murdered his ex-wife Nicole Brown and Ronald Goldman, had he done it. In the same light, perhaps Clinton can write a book outlining what the meaning of is is. Perhaps not since this man doesn't know that harass is on fact one word.

Sexual Harassment

The accusations that Anita Hill made against Clarence Thomas when he was being considered for a seat on the Supreme Court were nothing compared to what Clinton has been accused of by a number of women. To liberals and the National Association of Women, what Hill said was the gospel. Anybody that dared question Hill's motivation was immediately attacked. Women don't lie about something as serious as sexual harassment, and where there's smoke there's fire. A man even accused of sexual harassment is not qualified to hold such a responsible position in our government.

Now, compare that to the liberals' reactions to the women that accused

Clinton of unwanted sexual advances including a credible accusation of rape by

Juanita Broderick. Where was the National Organization of Women when James

Carville was calling Paula Jones trailer trash? This is such a stunning case of

liberal hypocrisy it's almost hard to believe it truly happened. Why isn't NOW

being considered a laughing stock for not defending the women harassed by

Clinton? Where is the media confronting Mrs. Bill Clinton about how this was all

true and was not in fact something that was dreamed up by the 'vast right-wing

conspiracy'.

Sandy Berger

The high and mighty Clintons also had no problem defending the actions

of Sandy Berger. Sandy Berger was the National Security Advisor to Bill Clinton.

This guy removed classified documents from the National Archives. He literally

stuffed papers downs his pants to steal them. He had the nerve to say he didn't

realize that he had the documents that they must have fallen into the trousers

without his knowledge. If there's anybody over the age of 3 that buys that lie I've

got some great ocean front property in Kansas I'd like to sell you.

Even if Mr. Berger had mistakenly removed the classified documents, he

could have returned them. Certainly the former NSA to a president would

understand the sensitive nature of classified documents and would want to return

them to the National Archives as soon as he discovered his 'honest' mistake.

Being that he did in fact destroy the documents, we'll never know exactly what

was taken. It doesn't take a leap of faith to believe that he was stealing documents damaging to the Clintons. This is why Mrs. Clinton remained quiet when it came to the criminal acts that Berger committed, but displayed righteous indignation at Bush's commutation of Libby's prison sentence. This woman truly has no shame.

It's even more outrageous for Mrs. Clinton to feign outrage over the commutation of Libby's sentence stating that the crime of lying under oath was so very serious. This is the woman whose husband shook his finger to the nation and swore (lied) that he never had sexual relations with that woman, Miss Lewinsky. This is the same Mrs. Clinton who while testifying before Congress about her role in Whitewater repeatedly said 'I don't recall'. This is the same Mrs. Clinton that miraculously found subpoenaed documents in the private residence of the White House two years after the fact.

The Clintons are congenital liars that will say and do anything in the name of power. For them to feign outrage at Bush's commuting Libby's sentence is a downright insult to the intelligence of the American people. I like what Tony Snow stated in response to Mrs. Clinton's outrage over the Libby issue - *"I don't know what Arkansan is for chutzpah, but this is a gigantic case of it,"*

When 8 is greater than 93

The Bush administration has fired 8 federal prosecutors. For this, the left is demanding answers and are calling for the resignation of Attorney General Alberto Gonzales. Here again, liberals need both a lesson in history as well as one in honesty. When Clinton took office, he fired all 93 federal prosecutors, yep each and every one of them one. While President Bush fired 8 federal prosecutors for cause, Clinton cleaned house. There had been Republicans in the White House for 12 years, and it was time for a change. There were also a lot of political cronies that were in need of good government jobs. Bill created 93 job vacancies with the stroke of a pen.

Filegate

Clinton wasted no time creating his pattern of corruption after taking the oath of office. In 1993, Craig Livingstone, who was the Director of the White House's Office of Personnel Security illegally obtained the FBI files on hundreds of Republicans. Livingstone testified that he didn't know that he was doing was wrong. Hell, this guy couldn't even remember who in the White House hired him to be the Director of Personnel Security. At a minimum, the Clintons need a better interviewing process so a bonehead like Livingstone doesn't get hired. This was no accident by an incompetent Craig Livingstone, this was a well orchestrated plan by the Clinton personal destruction machine to use (abuse) the power of the presidency in order to get dirt on anybody that was a potential political rival. I will now intertwine religion and politics and pray to heaven above that for the good of the country Mrs. Bill Clinton is not elected president.

Who's the Real Draft Dodger

The left has criticized George Bush for not serving in Vietnam. They have even stated that his joining the Texas Air National Guard was tantamount to dodging the draft, insinuating that nobody in the National Guard have ever seen any combat action. For the record, members of the National Guard did in fact see combat in Vietnam, just as they did in World War II, Korea, Desert Storm, and are now serving in Iraq. It is true that Bush himself never was deployed to Vietnam, and the liberals made a big case of that. This is so hypocritical that it's almost beyond the realm of human comprehension.

Bill Clinton was a real draft dodger. This is not the opinion of a conservative, but is a matter of historical fact. While people of good conscience can debate the merits of the Vietnam war, this future president protested against his own country while living in England. If that weren't enough, in a letter dated December 3, 1969, Clinton stated his true feelings about military service. In the letter Clinton wrote; *"No government really rooted in limited, parliamentary democracy should have the power to make its citizens fight and kill and die in a war they may oppose, a war which even possibly may be wrong, a war which, in any case, does not involve immediately the peace and freedom of the nation." Because of my opposition to the draft and the war. I am in great sympathy with those who are not willing to fight, kill and maybe die for their country (i.e. the particular policy of a particular government) right or wrong.*

As a service to the extreme left, I will remind them that America's involvement in Vietnam started under democrat John F. Kennedy. Many people that were of draft age in 1964 voted for Johnson because they were worried that Barry Goldwater would escalate the war. In fact, the democrats ran a particularly ugly campaign attack ad that year showing a little girl playing in a field of flowers getting nuked. Insinuating the dangers of voting for Goldwater. Of course history tells us that Lyndon Johnson did not bring a swift end to the Vietnam War. In fact just the opposite is true as he greatly escalated America's commitment. It was Richard Nixon, a Republican that got us out of Vietnam.

The Clinton's and the Military

The Clinton's so hate the military that marines stationed inside of the White House were not allowed to wear their uniforms while he was in office. That directive reportedly came from first lady and co-president Mrs. Bill Clinton. The Clinton's also feared our own military. Members of the military special forces units were ordered to keep their distance from Clinton. He was worried that they would try to assassinate him. That odor you're detecting is the smell of paranoia.

The left has stated that in the current struggle against terrorism, that our military is stretched to thin. During his eight years in office, Bill Clinton did more to weaken our military than any other president in recent history. Every branch of the military was cut way back. Between base closures and other actions this man took, he cut our military readiness by around 50%. Many people that joined the military under Ronald Reagan chose not to re-enlist under Clinton. Somehow serving under a man known as 'The Great Philanderer' or 'The Great Perjurer' was just not as inspiring as serving under 'The Great Communicator'.

Attacks on Success

With the exception of a conservative, there's nothing a liberal hates more than a successful business model. Their venom is not limited to Big Oil and Big Tobacco, during the Clinton years, Microsoft was in their crosshairs as well. Their attacks on Microsoft nearly caused the brake up of the world's largest software manufacturer. Love or hate Bill Gates, the company that he founded has greatly improved all of our lives. The overwhelming number of personal computers in use today work off of the Windows platform. Most of us that surf the Internet do so using Internet Explorer, a Microsoft product. Aside from the tens of thousands of employees that directly work for Microsoft, many more people have jobs that in one way or another are related to Gates' products. There are companies like Dell and Hewlett Packard that sell computers that use Microsoft software. Every company in the country that has a computer network of any reasonable size has computer engineers that support systems running Microsoft software.

The amount of wealth and opportunity that Bill Gates has created for millions of people across the globe is almost incalculable. A catch phrase back in the 90's was that Clinton was more concerned with 'Icons' than he was with the 'Chicoms' In other words, our command-n-chief saw more danger in Bill Gates than in China. I guess that's why he opted to give China missile technology and not Microsoft. Clinton is no more of a foreign policy expert than Jimmy Carter is.

Another widely successful business that is under attack from the left is Wal-Mart. Almost every time Wal-Mart opens a new store, the liberals are there to protest. They say that Wal-Mart doesn't pay their employees enough, and that too many of their employees are part-timers. Bear in mind that as a private sector business, Wal-Mart is not in a position to force anybody to work for them. In fact, just the opposite is true. When Wal-Mart conducts hiring for the opening of a new store, it is not unusual to get thousands of applicants for a couple of hundred jobs. It's been said that on a strictly percentage basis, you have better odds of getting accepted to Harvard than getting hired at a new Wal-Mart location.

Also consider that effect that Wal-Mart has on the local economies they have stores in. As an anchor store, many other businesses will be successful that open up near a Wal-Mart as a result of the increased customer traffic that is generated. State and local governments also see a huge influx in both sales and property tax revenues. Both the poor and the middle-class benefit from the low prices that Wal-Mart sells its products for. Somehow I doubt John Edwards buys his hair care products from Wal-Mart.

Healthcare

Perhaps what angers the left the most is Wal-Mart's recent program to sell prescription medicines for $4.00. Democrats always state that our nation's health care system is broken and needs a major overhaul. *(Liberal to English translation – they actually mean socialized medicine)* They often state that many people on fixed incomes have to choose between their medicines and whether or not to eat. So, when Wal-Mart started selling prescription medicines for $4.00, you'd think the left would welcome this with open arms. After all, Wal-Mart is providing low cost prescription medicines to people, without the need for any taxation or government intervention. The truth is that liberals aren't interested in providing people with low cost medicines. They are interested in creating a huge new entitlement program that will cost billions of tax payer dollars that will be less effective than what Wal-Mart is doing today.

Hillary-Care was the dream child of Mrs. Bill Clinton. A socialized system that was so extreme that her own party voted against it back in 1994. This woman's plan was so leftist that it was credited with being one of the reasons that the Republicans won a majority in both houses of Congress for the first time in 40 years in the '94 mid-term elections. Socialized healthcare would bankrupt this country. On the way to bankruptcy, the quality of healthcare would go from where it is now, to be on par with Cuba. We spend billions of dollars every year now for free healthcare for the estimate 10 – 12 million illegals in this country. Imagine what the cost would be to try and cover 300 million people.

If you want to have a sense of just how crazy Hillary-Care would be, just take a look at San Francisco. That bastion of left-wing lunacy actually pays to cover the expenses of city employees to have sex change operations. The city tax payers of San Francisco are forced to pay the over $30,000 costs to have some guy have his tally whacker cut off. It costs even more money to attach one to a woman who wants to pretend to be a guy. Why is the song 'Lola' by The Kinks going through my mind right now?

Beyond the obvious lunacy of San Francisco, if people wants to pierce their lips, nipples, genitals, tongues or whatever else they're doing today, I don't feel the need for my tax dollars going to cover the costs if they get an infection. Now, I'm not saying that they should be denied medical care, but if you live a risky lifestyle, you should assume the liabilities. Of course, personal responsibility is a concept completely foreign to liberals.

Perform a Google search for countries where patients have had their operations cancelled. You will see a direct correlation to countries that have socialized medicine. It has been a miserable failure everywhere it's been tried. People in countries such as England, Canada and France are literally dying while waiting to receive medical care. Look at the last sentence again we're not talking about 3rd world hell holes that are 100 years behind us in medical science. We're talking about technologically advanced countries where their citizens are dying because of the failure of their respective socialized health care systems.

Hillary-Care would have socialized roughly 1/7 of the country's economy. It would have empowered government bureaucrats with the ability to tell us which doctors we were allowed to see. For those who believe that the government would be efficient at running a national healthcare system, check out veterans' hospitals.

When liberals state that millions of Americans don't have health insurance, they are greatly inflating the numbers. Consider a household where both the husband and wife work outside the home. The employer provided health benefits for one spouse may be better than those of the other. So, the 'second' spouse may opt not to participate in the health insurance provided by their company. Liberals would count that person as being uninsured even though they were covered by their spouse's health insurance.

Hillary-Care would also have made it illegal for Americans to seek private doctors. Let that sink in for a minute. Under this woman's utopia, it would have been a crime to try and use your own private funds to go to a doctor of your own choosing. Does this sound like value's that made our country great?

Are there problems with our healthcare system today? The obvious answer is yes there is. Costs are way too high and frivolous lawsuits are certainly not helping. Along those lines, consider what has had a more positive effect on the overall healthcare situation, Wal-Mart offering $4.00 prescriptions, or John Edwards enriching himself by conducting a nutty séance as part of his lawsuit forcing doctors to perform unneeded C-sections.. Also bear in mind that socialized medicine has not been a success anywhere it has been tried. The truth is that socialism has failed in every instance that it has been tried. To a liberal, it's not that socialism is a bad system it's that they haven't been allowed to run it yet.

Democrats and Dependency

Liberals truly believe that our country would be better off by adopting a socialist economy versus our current free market model. Actually, democrats want to create as much dependency on government as they possibly can. To be even more specific, they believe that socialism is what is best for the rest of us. We the unclean masses that live in fly-over country are far too ignorant to be allowed to live our lives with a degree of self-reliance. However, limousine liberals have no intentions of sending their kids to public schools, or being confined by the restrictions of Hillary-Care. That's for the rest of us. Could you imagine what John Edwards would do if the left ever instituted government operated barber shops? He'd have to travel to Canada to get his hair cut.

Liberals will say things like we don't spend enough money on research to fight HIV and AIDS. The truth is that the government spends more money on research on both HIV and AIDS than it does for any other illness. This is despite the fact that far more people die of heart disease and cancer than they do of HIV or AIDS. Since HIV and AIDS is a disease spread by unprotected gay sex and drug users sharing dirty needles, it's the perfect candidate for liberals to spend billions of tax payer dollars on to try and combat.

Now bear in mind that they don't preach protected sex, or monogamy amongst the gay community, or not share dirty needles with your drug buddies. After all, that would be making a value judgment. Rather than promote behaviors that would truly curtail the spread of a truly awful, and preventable disease, the left chooses the PC route.

Liberals will also say that more money needs to be spent on disease that effect women, in essence making the argument that the government not only doesn't care about gays, but doesn't care about women either. The truth is the more women die of heart disease than from breast cancer. Also, more government money goes to breast cancer research than is spent on fighting prostate cancer. Don't get me wrong, I am not advocating cutting back on research to find a cure for breast cancer. I'm just pointing out liberal lies and scare tactics. Make no mistake if voted into office President, Mrs. Bill Clinton will revive Hillary-Care.

Chapter #10

Abortion

Another non-existent Constitutional right invented by the extreme left was the right for women to kill their unborn babies. Since the 1973 Supreme Court decision in Roe v. Wade, some 40 million abortions have been performed in the United States. To the left, as with many of their issues, there is no middle ground. Anybody that mentions anything to the left of abortions on demand until the moment of delivery is viciously attacked.

Baby versus Tissue Mass

Liberals can't agree whether a fetus is an unborn baby or merely a mass of tissue. Liquor companies have been sued by women that have drank excessive amounts of alcohol during their pregnancies resulting in birth defects in their children. People that have killed pregnant women often face two counts of murder, one for the women, and another for her unborn child. So, in some cases, liberals have a sense that pregnant women are in fact carrying unborn children and not just a mass of tissue. I wonder if liberals ever attend baby showers? If what the expectant woman is carrying is nothing more than a tissue mass, what is there to celebrate?

Other the other hand, liberals will fight to the death to allow women to abort their children at any time during their pregnancy. We're not talking about cases having to do with rape, or the health/life of the mother. In many cases, abortions are done as an after the fact form of contraception. Bill Clinton couldn't even find enough goodness in his soul to sign bills that were sent to his desk to ban partial birth abortion. This is when a viable fetus, has its brains sucked out after it has been partially delivered. In no case is a partial birth abortion performed to save the life of the mother.

Abortion clinics such as Planned Parenthood don't even counsel expectant mothers on other options such as adoption. Nobody wants to cause expectant mothers unnecessary amounts of grief. However, in the long run, which decision do you think a woman will find easier to live with. Killing her unborn child, or giving it a chance for life by giving it up for adoption?

The Séance by John Edwards

John Edwards, another poster child for liberal hypocrisy, made millions suing doctors for not performing enough C-sections claiming they had caused brain damage and other birth defects. In fact, having supernatural powers akin to John Kerry's ability to cure Christopher Reeve, in 1985 John Edwards stood before a jury and channeled the words of an unborn baby girl. Referring to an hour-by-hour record of a fetal heartbeat monitor, Mr. Edwards told the jury: "She said at 3, `I'm fine.' She said at 4, `I'm having a little trouble, but I'm doing O.K.' Five, she said, `I'm having problems.' At 5:30, she said, `I need out.' As a result of his séance, Edwards made millions off of the verdict. Doctors perform for more C-sections now in fear of an Edward's style lawsuit. A C-section does cause greater pain to the mother. It also raises the cost of medical care, and has not been shown to have any reduction in the occurrence of birth defects. So, the price of medical care goes up, Edward's got rich and women are subjected to unnecessary C-sections. Hey Mrs. Clinton – socialized medicine is not the answer. However, reducing the number of multi-million dollar lawsuits enriching lawyers like Edwards would be a major step in the right direction. I wonder how Edwards was able to pay for his $1,200 haircuts prior to making millions off of his bogus lawsuit.

The Stem Cell Lie

One of the liberal's latest lies is to insist that human embryos must be destroyed in order that their stem cells can be harvested for medical research. To date, there have been no medical benefits found by using embryonic stem cells. However, the stem cells from umbilical cord fluid have shown great promise in helping with a wide range of very serious medical conditions. Adult stem cells have also shown more promise than embryonic stem cells. The great lie is that to a liberal, the cause is to promote more abortions, and not further the research of stem cell use to ease human suffering.

While I am a fan of Michael J. Fox as an actor, his television ads during the 2004 campaign were a disgrace. Fox suffers from Parkinson's disease. Of course, my heart goes out to any person suffering from that or any kind of difficult illness. However, Fox misled the nation by not taking the medicines that he has to help him control his tremors. Also, research that may ultimately cure Fox and others with Parkinson's are much more likely to come from umbilical cord stem cells than those from human embryos. He was using his disease to try and effect a political election and not help those suffering from difficult illnesses. Of course, who could forget the liberal's claim that if Kerry were elected president in 2004 that Christopher Reeve would be instantly cured and walk again. When you consider the fact that Mr. Reeve passed away in 2004 before the election, he was beyond even the supernatural powers of John Kerry.

Medical Science Determines the Beginning of Life

Liberals have stated that the reason a fetus has no right to life is that it can't survive outside of the mother. However, with each passing year advances in medical science push back the time into a pregnancy when a pre-mature child can in fact be saved. Preemies are being saved today that would have had no chance for survival 10 years ago. Unborn babies have been aborted in this country far after they had reached the point of viability by today's medical standards.

Furthermore, a newborn that is 2 hours old can't very well survive without its mother, or some adult caring for it either. A new born is no more able to care for itself than a fetus that is 8 ½ months along in its gestation period is. Talk to a woman that has ever had a miscarriage or given birth to a child that was still-born. Ask them if they feel that they have lost a child. The liberal's stance on abortion in many instances is tantamount to infanticide. For those of you in Rio Linda, that's when you murder an infant. *(Dittos Rush)* Liberals state that they are the champions of the poor and powerless. Who is more powerless than the unborn? They can't advocate for themselves, despite the circus act that was John Edwards. Remember, at one point in our existence, we were all pro-life. The unborn need the support of those of us whose parents felt that life was a better choice for us than abortion.

I find it astonishing that if you were to kill an unborn baby eagle, the liberals will throw you in prison. Now, I have nothing against unborn eagles, but aren't unborn humans at least on part with an unborn bird? Heaven help us is they ever find a way to determine if the fetus is a conservative.

Chapter #11

Liberals and Race

To a liberal, race relations in the United States are not far removed from where they were during either the early 1860's or even the early 1960's. Now, as a nation, have we done things in the past that were wrong? The honest answer is that of course we have. Slavery is a disgusting practice that no civilized people should ever practice or condone. Slavery in this country was such a divisive issue that we fought a civil war over it.

A Quick History Lesson

While liberals will say that they are the party best for minorities, bear in mind that is was southern DEMOCRATS that were the party that supported slave ownership. It was also Republican President Abraham Lincoln that was known as "The Great Emancipator" for freeing the slaves. Well into the 20th century, it was southern DEMOCRATS that championed many of the segregation in this country. It was also democrats that wanted to count blacks as only 4/5 of a person when it came to the census.

Having separate bathrooms for whites and blacks was not something that Republicans came up with. Republicans in the north didn't have public restaurants that were off limits to blacks, as was common place in the south. Even as recently as the Hurricane Katrina tragedy, liberals tried to say that the lack of response from the federal government was because Republicans don't care about the plight of blacks. The real truth is that Katrina and the FEMA response showed the inefficiency of a federal bureaucracy to deal with a disaster of that magnitude. Katrina was also a glaring example of what happens when a city is governed by liberals for 40 years. Levies don't get reinforced, and an entire city is almost destroyed. It also shows what happens when people get so dependent on government that they don't even have enough of a sense of self-reliance to flee from a hurricane.

New Orleans Representative, Democratic William Jefferson, a black man, was more concerned about retrieving the $90,000 that he had in his freezer than helping his constituents. I also find it stunning that he was re-elected even after it was revealed that he that much 'cold' hard cash in his freezer. What the heck, Marion Berry was re-elected as the mayor of Washington D.C. even after it was common knowledge that he regularly used cocaine.

Liberal's Effect on Minorities

Minorities are impacted the most by the liberal monopoly of the school system. On the whole, most inner-city schools are the worst in the nation. It is not uncommon for children to be promoted from grade to grade, and given a high school diploma without learning the 3 R's. Liberals have even stated that blacks youths shouldn't be expected to learn what most would consider a learned level of English, because they speak 'Ebonics'. Ebonics is being promoted by liberals as the native language of African Americans. There are no blacks in Africa that are speaking Ebonics. Ebonics is merely a dialect common to African American youths. It would be akin to saying that whites in the south shouldn't be required to learn proper English because their native language is 'Red Neck'. According to the Journal of Black Education, over the past 20 years the gap between the average SAT scores for blacks and whites has increased. The scores have gone down for both groups, with the scores for blacks declining faster than those of whites. The public school system is not helping blacks attain the level of education that will help them obtain their personal goals.

Effective Education – The Bane of Liberalism

Black people speaking 'Ebonics' are not going to get high paying, professional jobs that will help lift them out of the depths of poverty. Liberals know this, and the truth is that they want blacks to stay poor. Liberals have built a huge voting block that is dependent on black poverty. Democrats have benefited tremendously from their creation of multi-generational welfare recipients. On a regular basis, blacks vote overwhelmingly democrat. If effective education was ever introduced into inner-city black communities, it would represent a huge threat to liberals. Why do you think liberals dislike successful blacks such as; Clarence Thomas, Condoleezza Rice, Colin Powell and Bill Cosby. They are all highly educated, extremely successful and worst of all, they aren't liberal.

The truth of the matter is that the black community would benefit greatly from conservative initiatives. Easing regulations and lowering corporate taxes would provide incentives for businesses to move into the inner-cities. The creation of such enterprise zones would produce badly needed jobs and opportunity. Both the poor and minorities would also benefit the most from school vouchers. Education, and the self reliance that it gives you, is the best way to lift yourself out of poverty. Liberals of course prefer multi-generational welfare recipients going through life at the poverty line. Just as long as they keep voting them into office, the liberals will keep them alive, barely.

Liberals often will say that conservatives don't care about women or minorities. It was Ronald Reagan a Republican that nominated the first woman to the United States Supreme Court. President Bush has had more minorities in senior positions in his administration than Clinton had in his. Colin Powell, Condoleezza Rice and Alberto Gonzales all have had very senior roles in Bush's administration.

Diversity and Quotas

Dr. Martin Luther King Jr. prayed for a day when people would be measured not by the color of their skin, but by the content of their character. Dr. King was truly a great man. It is unfortunate that liberals are the ones that promote race-based policies. In many instances, decisions regarding hiring and university admissions are based more on skin color than on merit. Was there a time when race-based quotas were needed to make up for the wrongs of the past? That is a question that many can debate. For now, it is safe to say that none of the white males looking for a job today were discriminating against blacks 40 years ago before the signing of the 1967 Civil Rights Act.

Anybody still alive that had a job back then is either at or very near retirement today. For liberals, enough is never enough. Companies have been sued for not having a work force that had the identical racial makeup of the surrounding community. It didn't matter if certain ethnicities didn't apply or were unqualified. Race-based quotas have in effect created situations where the sign might as well read 'whites males need not apply'.

Diversity to a liberal is based strictly on skin color and gender. Well to be fair you'd want to through in factors such as sexual orientation and physical disability. If you want to build a strong team, you should look for diversity of relevant knowledge and experience. As an example, if you wanted to build a team that could work on any kind of computer, you'd want people with diverse knowledge to be able to work on UNIX, Windows, Mainframes, mid-range computers, firewalls and more. That would be the kind of diversity that you should be looking for. When putting such a team together, or any team for that matter, skin color shouldn't be a determining factor.

The Impact of Racial Quotas

Some of the unintended consequences of racial quotas include minorities being placed in responsible positions for which they are not qualified. If these positions are to benefit other people of color, these minorities could be disadvantaged because of the inefficiency of the unqualified worker. Doesn't our government owe us a duty to hire the best people that they can to fill jobs in their bureaucracies? After all, their salaries are being paid for by our tax dollars.

Another unintended consequence is that highly qualified minorities are sometimes accused of not really earning their jobs, that it was just handed to them to fill a race-based quota. I find it interesting that liberals will accuse white males of not having to work to get the jobs that they land. The last time that I checked, being a white male didn't earn you any points on a job application.

However, in some instances, being a minority is worth more points on a job application than having a relevant advanced university degree. Racial quotas also work off of the premise that either the individual or their descendants were the direct victims of racism. However, if a minority were to come into the United States this year, they would benefit from racial quotas. Never mind that they had not lived in the United States before and had never suffered from the racism that was prevalent in the south.

These practices also have the effect of punishing white males for the 'crimes' of their ancestors. That's assuming they come from a lineage of southern democrat slave owners. What about caucasians that recently immigrated into this country and never had anything to do with the unfair racial practices of the past? Is it fair that their children should be punished for things that occurred before they even came to this country? I'm sure that had the 2007 illegal immigration bill had passed, the 12 million illegal aliens would be given priority over American citizens that happened to be while males in both hiring and university admissions. I'd like to believe that I've made my point. That being that racial quotas benefits nobody except for liberals preying on the fears of minorities telling them that they won't get a job unless they keep voting democrat.

There is almost no business or government bureaucracy that is immune from these types of racial quotas. There are of course a couple of notable exceptions. Professions that are considered so critical that liberals understand that rather than making hiring decisions based on race, that only highly qualified individuals should be considered. Can you guess what these professions are? If you guessed professional sports, you're correct. There are no gender, race or age quotas there. If there were, as a 5'7" white male in my 40's, I'd have a heck of a law suit against the NBA.

Don Imus

Don Imus had the title of 'shock jock'. His would say things on his radio show that some would consider shocking. OK – that's what a shock jock does. Here in a supposedly free country, you can choose to listen to what Imus has to say or not. When he called members of the Rutgers University women's basketball team a bunch of 'nappy headed hoes', all hell broke loose. Now, is what he said demeaning and inappropriate? Sure, and in fact in certain circles it can be considered downright racist and sexist. However, the lyrics in much of Rap music sung by both black and white so called 'artists' is far worse than anything Imus has said on the air. Why aren't the keepers of what can and can't be uttered on the airways attacking them? Why did Jesse Jackson and Al Sharpton make it their mission to make certain that Imus lost his job? Where is their righteous indignation when Robert 'kkk' Byrd uses the 'N' word?

It's not that I want to hear the type of things that a shock jock like Imus has to say. I'm not particularly interested in that type of 'entertainment' so I don't listen to it. Apparently enough people were listening to Imus to make his program successful. Now, Air America wasn't the most complimentary radio program when talking about conservatives. They went off of the air not because of protests caused by the inflammatory statements, but because nobody listened to them.

Innocents were Attacked

One of the reasons that liberals use to say why what Imus said was so bad is the fact that the women of the Rutgers basketball team were private citizens and hence should be off-limits for this type of verbal assault. Where are the liberals coming to the defense of the Duke Lacrosse players? These young boys were also innocents. They were falsely accused of rape, and were the subject of both an out of control prosecutor and mean spirited liberal professors. Mike Nifong prosecuted these poor boys long after any reasonable attorney should have concluded that they were innocent. His conduct was so unprofessional that he has since been removed from office. Where are the apologizes from the 88 Duke University professors that accused these poor boys of rape long before the facts of the case were able to come out? Apparently none of the professors were schooled in our nation's form of jurisprudence that says that people are presumed innocent until proven guilty. I guarantee you that the hell that these kids had to endure for a year as the case unfolded was far worse than the embarrassment Imus caused the young ladies at Rutgers.

Summary

Well, we've reached the end of what I hope has been both an informative and enjoyable read. I've tried to point of much of the hypocrisy of the left. It is my no means a comprehensive list, and every day seems to bring new subject matter to write about. I also intertwined the facts that I've presented with a certain level of satirical humor. This is not to make light of what are very serious topics facing our nation, but rather to use humor as an educational aide. Having read more than my share of text books in my day, I wanted to make sure my writings weren't as dry.

So thank you and keep the faith. We need to keep speaking out for what is right for our country. It won't be what the Hollywood types want to hear, and it won't get you a guest spot on the Evening News, but it is the right thing to do.

Appendix A

Pardons Granted by Bill Clinton

Source: U.S. Department of Justice's Website.

NAME	DISTRICT	SENTENCED	OFFENSE
November 23, 1994			
David Phillip Aronsohn	D. Minn.	1961	Failure to pay special occupational tax on wagering, 26 U.S.C. § 7203
Wanda Kaye Bain-Prentice	D. Ariz.	1982	Mail fraud, 18 U.S.C. § 1341
Antonio Barucco	U. S. Army general court-martial	1945	Desertion in violation of the 58th Article of War
Kristine Margo Beck	D. Idaho	1981	Bank embezzlement, 18 U.S.C. § 656
David Christopher Billmaier	D. New Mex.	1980	Possession with intent to distribute amphetamines, 21 U.S.C. § 841(a)(1)
Terry Lee Brown	E. D. Ky.	1962	Interstate transportation of a stolen motor vehicle, 18 U.S.C. § 2312
Joe Carl Bruton	N. D. Tex.	1979	Conspiracy to commit mail fraud, 18 U.S.C. § 371
Nolan Lynn DeMarce	W. D. Wis.	1983	Making false statements to obtain bank loans, 18 U.S.C. § 1014
Jimmy C. Dick	N. D. Calif.	1976	Conspiracy to manufacture counterfeit Federal Reserve Notes, 18 U.S.C. § 371
Edward Eugene Dishman	W. D. Okla.	1983	Conspiracy to defraud the United States and Oklahoma counties, 18 U.S.C. § 371
Brenda Kay Engle	S. D. Ind.	1983	Conspiracy to commit theft from interstate shipment, 18 U.S.C. § 371
Mary Theresa Fajer	D. Oregon	1980	Conspiracy to commit bank embezzlement, 18 U.S.C. §§ 2 and 371
Albert James Forte	D. Dist. Col.	1973	Making and subscribing false and fraudulent income tax return, 26 U.S.C. § 7206(1)
Fendley Lee Frazier	S. D. Ala.	1965	Interstate transportation of a stolen motor vehicle, 18 U.S.C. § 2312
Robert Linward Freeland, Jr.	N. D. Ind.	1983	Forcible rescue of seized property, 26 U.S.C. § 7212(b)

Ralph Leon Furst	S. D. Calif.	1966	Embezzlement of United States mail (U.S. Code section not cited)
Barbara Ann Gericke	W. D. Wis.	1984	Conspiracy to introduce contraband into federal prison, 18 U.S.C. §§ 371 and 1791
Billy Joe Gilmore	N. D. Tex.	1982	Mail fraud and aiding and abetting, 18 U.S.C. §§ 1341 and 2
Loreto Joseph Iafrate	N. D. W. Va.	1976	Failure to record receipt of firearms, 18 U.S.C. §§ 922(m) and 924(a)
Carl Bruce Jones	W. D. Mo.	1983	Distribution of marijuana and use of telephone to facilitate marijuana distribution, 18 U.S.C. § 2 and 21 U.S.C. §§ 841(a)(1) and 843(b)
Candace Deon Leverenz	N. D. Calif.	1972	Unlawful distribution of LSD, 21 U.S.C. §§ 841(a)(1) and (b)(1)(B)
George William Lindgren	S. D. N. Y.	1975	Bank embezzlement, 18 U.S.C. § 656
Brian George Meierkord	C. D. Ill.	1983	Making false statement to bank, 18 U.S.C. § 1014
Jackie Lee Miller	N. D. Okla.	1983	Conspiracy to defraud the United States, 18 U.S.C. § 371
Joseph Patrick Naulty	E. D. Pa.	1980	Carrying away goods moving as part of foreign shipment, 18 U.S.C. § 659
Theodore Roosevelt Noel	N. D. Ala.	1972	Selling whiskey in unstamped containers and making false statement in the acquisition of firearms from licensed dealer, 26 U.S.C. § 5604(a)(1) and 18 U.S.C. §§ 922(a)(6) and 924(a)
Mary Louise Oaks	M. D. La.	1979	Conspiracy to defraud the government with respect to claims, 18 U.S.C. § 286
Robert Paul Padelsky	D. Utah	1980	Misapplication of bank funds, 18 U.S.C. § 656
Elizabeth Amy Peterson	D. Nev.	1985	Conspiracy to make false statements to bank, 18 U.S.C. § 371
Susan Lauranne Prather	W. D. Ark.	1975	Causing marijuana to be transported through the mail, 21 U.S.C. § 843(b)
Gary Lynn Quammen	W. D. Wis.	1976	Misapplication of bank funds, 18 U.S.C. § 656
Robert Ronal Raymond	D. Conn.	1972	Conspiracy to manufacture, receive, possess, and sell firearms silencers, 18 U.S.C. § 371
Elizabeth Hogg Rushing	N. D. Ga.	1978	Misapplication of bank funds, 18 U.S.C. § 656
Marc Alan Schaffer	S. D. N. Y.	1968	Submission of false statements to Selective Service System Local Board, 50 U.S.C. Appendix § 462(a)
Roy Aaron Smith	E. D. Tex.	1982	Misprision of a felony, 18 U.S.C. § 4

Diane Dorothea Smunk	D. So. Dak.	1984	Embezzlement by government employee, 18 U.S.C. § 641
Thomas Peter Stathakis	D. So. Car.	1976	Selling and delivering firearms to out-of-state resident and falsifying firearms records, 18 U.S.C. §§ 922(b)(3), 922(m), and 924(a)
Kathleen Vacanti	C. D. Calif.	1979	Conspiracy to defraud the United States by obtaining payment of false claims, presenting false claims to the United States, forging a writing, and aiding and abetting, 18 U.S.C. §§ 2, 286, 287, and 495
Pupi White	W. D. Mo.	1985	Making false statement on United States passport application, 18 U.S.C. § 911
Charles Coleman Wicker	E. D. Mo.	1975	Conspiracy to conduct illegal gambling business, 18 U.S.C. § 371
Roderick Douglas Woods	S. D. Miss.	1982	Misappropriation of bank funds and aiding and abetting, 18 U.S.C. §§ 656 and 2

April 17, 1995			
NAME	DISTRICT	SENTENCED	OFFENSE
Bradley Vaughn Barisic	N. D. Calif.	1980	Making false statement to National Labor Relations Board, 18 U.S.C. § 1001
Herschel L. Brantley	U. S. Air Force general court-martial	1951	Larceny in violation of 93rd Article of War
Linda Bailey Byars	D. So. Car.	1975	Bank embezzlement, 18 U.S.C. § 656
Patricia Ann Chapin	W. D. Mo.	1986	Falsifying prescription for controlled substance, 21 U.S.C. § 843(a)(4)(A) and 18 U.S.C. § 2
Ronald Jacobs	E. D. Pa.	1967	Theft from interstate shipment, 18 U.S.C. § 659
Margaret Mary Marks	N. D. Ohio	1984	Willful misapplication of bank funds, 18 U.S.C. § 657
John Richard Martin	S. D. Calif.	1956	Embezzlement of funds from savings and loan association, 18 U.S.C. § 657
Earl Thomas McKinney	1. U. S. Air Force summary court-martial	1. 1951	Absent without leave
	2. U. S. Air Force general court-martial	2. 1959	Larceny by check, writing check with insufficient funds, and false claims, in violation of U.C.M.J. Articles 121, 132, and 134
Shirley Jean	S. D. Tex.	1978	Filing false claim for tax refund, 18 U.S.C. § 287

Odoms			
Jack Pakis	W. D. Ark.	1972	Operation of illegal gambling business, 18 U.S.C. §§ 2 and 1955
Gordon Roberts, Jr.	M. D. La.	1977	Interstate transportation of forged and falsely made securities, 18 U.S.C. §§ 2 and 2314
Carl Edward Terhune, Jr.	N. D. Okla.	1985	Issuing United States Postal Service money orders while postal employee with intent to defraud Postal Service, 18 U.S.C. § 500

December 23, 1997			
NAME	DISTRICT	SENTENCED	OFFENSE
Irving Frank Avery	D. Colo.	1984	Possession of counterfeit plates, 18 U.S.C. §§ 474 and 2
Billy K. Berry	E. D. Ark.	1986	Medicaid and mail fraud, 42 U.S.C. § 1396h(a)(1)(i) and 18 U.S.C. § 1341
Clio Louise Carson	D. Wyo.	1979	Transmission of wagering information, 18 U.S.C. § 1084
Giuseppe Casadei-Severei	D. Puerto Rico	1987	Obstruction of justice, 18 U.S.C. § 1503
Glen Edison Chapman	1. W. D. No.Car.	1. 1955	Removing, possessing, and concealing non-tax-paid whiskey, 26 U.S.C. §§ 5632 and 7206
	2. W. D. No. Car.	2. 1957	Removing, possessing, and concealing non-tax-paid whiskey, 26 U.S.C. §§ 5632 and 5008(b)(1)
Ralph Wallace Crawford	C. D. Calif.	1985	Mail fraud, 18 U.S.C. § 1341
Aaron Golden	W. D. Tex.	1986	Failure to file a currency transaction report, 31 U.S.C. §§ 5313 and 5322(a)
Monroe Lee King	S. D. Tex.	1973	Making plates for counterfeiting Federal Reserve Notes, 18 U.S.C. § 474
Ralph Lee Limbaugh	N. D. Ala.	1974	Theft from interstate shipment, 18 U.S.C. § 659
George Edward Maynes, Jr.	D. Canal Zone	1975	Distribution of cocaine, 21 U.S.C. § 841(a)(1)
Charley Morgan	N.D. Okla.	1964	Unlawful possession of still and manufacture of mash, 26 U.S.C. §§ 5179(a), 5601(a)(1), and 5601(a)(7)
Linzie Murle Morse	W. D. La.	1973	Interstate transportation of stolen motor vehicle and selling stolen motor vehicle, 18 U.S.C. §§ 2312 and 2313
Charles Patrick Murrin	C. D. Calif.	1988	Bank robbery, 18 U.S.C. § 2113(a)
Moises Jaurequi Ramos	D. New Mexico	1983	Misprision of a felony, 18 U.S.C. § 4
William Ray	W. D. Mo.	1983	Interstate transportation of stolen property, 18

Richardson			U.S.C. §§ 2 and 2314
Raymond Phillip Weaver	U. S. Navy summary court-martial	1947	Theft of four pounds of butter
Bill Wayne West	E. D. Miss.	1984	Dealing in firearms without license, 18 U.S.C. §§ 922(a)(1) and 924(a)
Anita Glenn Whitlock	D. Dist. Col.	1978	Bank embezzlement, 18 U.S.C. § 656
Edward Kenneth Williams, Jr.	S. D. Iowa	1979	Receiving and selling stolen motor vehicles and aiding and abetting the same, 18 U.S.C. §§ 2 and 2313
Larry Edward Winfield	W. D. Ark.	1987	Mail fraud, 18 U.S.C. § 1341
Louis Anthony Winters	1. U.S. Navy general court-martial	1. 1957	1. Unauthorized absence from duty
	2.D. So. Dak.	2. 1969	2. Assault with dangerous weapon, 18 U.S.C. § 1153

December 24, 1998			
NAME	DISTRICT	SENTENCED	OFFENSE
Haig Ardash Arakelian (aka Haig Arthur Arakelian)	S. D. Calif.	1975	Possession of marijuana, 21 U.S.C. § 844
Estel Edmond Ashworth	N. D. Tex.	1974	Theft of mail by Postal employee, 18 U.S.C. § 1709
Vincent Anthony Burgio	C. D. Calif.	1972	Possession of counterfeit government obligations, 18 U.S.C. § 472
Thomas Earl Burton	E. D. Va.	1982	Attempted possession with intent to distribute cocaine, 21 U.S.C. §§ 841(a)(1) and 846
Jesse Cuevas	D. Neb.	1984	Unauthorized possession of food stamps, 7 U.S.C. § 2024(b)
Harry Erla Fox	U.S. Army summary and special courts-martial	1961	Absence without leave, Article 86, U.C.M.J.
James William Gardner	D. Wyo.	1983	Conspiracy to distribute cocaine, 21 U.S.C. §§ 846 and 841(a)(1)
Alejandro Cruz Guedea	U.S. Army general	1949	Larceny of government property

	court-martial		
Sebraien Michael Haygood	E. D. N. Y.	1982	Importation of cocaine, 21 U.S.C. §§ 952(a) and 960(a)(1)
Warren Curtis Hultgren, Jr.	W. D. Tex.	1982	Conspiracy to possess with intent to distribute cocaine, 21 U.S.C. §§ 846 and 841(a)(1)
Sharon Sue Johnson	E. D. Ark.	1986	Bank embezzlement, 18 U.S.C. § 656
Ronald Ray Kelly	U.S. Marine Corps special court-martial	1969	Unauthorized absences, escape from lawful custody, and breaking restriction
Francis Dale Knippling	D. So. Dak.	1985	Conversion of mortgaged property, 18 U.S.C. § 658
Michael Ray Krukar	D. Alaska	1988	Unlawful distribution of marijuana, 21 U.S.C. § 841(a)(1)
Michael Francis Larkin	D. Mass.	1984	False statements to HUD, 18 U.S.C. §§ 2 and 1001
Leslie Jan McCall	W. D. Okla.	1988	Use of telephone to facilitate cocaine distribution, 21 U.S.C. § 843(b)
Bobby Joe Miller	E. D. Tex.	1982	Misprision of a felony, 18 U.S.C. § 4
William Edward Payne	D. Ore.	1965	Willful attempt to evade excise tax on wagers, 26 U.S.C. § 7201
Robert Earl Radke	C. D. Calif.	1981	Willful attempt to evade income taxes, 26 U.S.C. § 7201
David Walter Ratliff	N. D. Okla.	1981	Making false statement to the government, 18 U.S.C. § 1001
Billy Wayne Reynolds	E. D. Tex.	1981	Mail fraud, 18 U.S.C. § 1341
Benito Maldonado Sanchez, Jr.	W. D. Tex.	1960	Possession of marijuana without payment of transfer tax, 26 U.S.C. § 4744(1)
Vicki Lynn Seals (fka Vicki Lynn Miller)	W. D. Tex.	1984	Making a false statement to a federally insured bank while an employee of that bank, 18 U.S.C.§ 1005
Lewis Craig Seymour	W. D. Okla.	1979	Distribution of Phencyclidine (PCP), 21 U.S.C. § 841(a)(1)
Irving A. Smith	D. Md.	1957	Conspiracy to engage in price-fixing, 15 U.S.C. §§ 1 and 2 (Sherman Act)
Darrin Paul Sobin	E. D. Calif.	1987	Conspiracy to manufacture marijuana, 21 U.S.C. § 841(a)(1)

Monty Mac Stewart	W. D. Okla.	1983	Conspiracy to defraud U.S. and counties within Oklahoma, mail fraud, and aiding and abetting filing a false income tax return, 18 U.S.C. §§ 2, 371, and 1341, and 26 U.S.C. § 7206(1)
Kevin Lester Teker	W. D. Wash.	1989	Maliciously damaging property used in an activity affecting interstate commerce by means of an explosive, 18 U.S.C. § 844(i)
John Timothy Thompson	W. D. Okla.	1986	Use of the telephone to facilitate cocaine distribution, 21 U.S.C. § 843(b)
Paul Loy Tobin	S. D. Ala.	1968	Interstate transportation of stolen motor vehicle, 18 U.S.C. § 2312
Gerald William Wachter	E. D. Pa.	1974	Conspiracy to cause stolen goods to be transported in interstate commerce, 18 U.S.C. § 371
Marian Lane Wolf	N. D. Tex.	1988	Misprision of a felony, 18 U.S.C. § 4
Samuel Harrell Woodard	1. U.S. Air Force summary court-martial	1. 1952	1. Absent without leave
	2. S. D. Ga.	2. 1955	2. Theft from an interstate shipment, 18 U.S.C. § 659

February 19, 1999			
NAME	**DISTRICT**	**SENTENCED**	**OFFENSE**
Henry Ossian Flipper	U.S. Army general court-martial	1891	Conduct unbecoming an officer

December 23, 1999			
NAME	**DISTRICT**	**SENTENCED**	**OFFENSE**
Meredith Marcus Appleton, II	W. D. Okla.	1990	Conspiracy to possess with intent to distribute cocaine and to distribute cocaine, 21 U.S.C. § 846
Steven Laurence Barnett	E. D. Calif.	1987	Misapplication of bank funds and aiding and abetting the same, 18 U.S.C. §§ 2 and 657
Russell Carl Clifton	N. D. Calif.	1977	Transmission of a false distress signal, 47 U.S.C. § 325 (misdemeanor)
Albert McMullen Cox	S. D. Ga.	1987	Bribery of a public official, 18 U.S.C. § 201(b)
Bernard Earl Crandall	C. D. Ill.	1985	Theft from interstate shipment, 18 U.S.C. § 659
Eugene Harold Del Carlo	N. D. Calif.	1979	Conspiracy and blackmail, 18 U.S.C. §§ 371 and 873 (misdemeanors)

Kenneth Lee Deusterman	D. Minn.	1991	False statement to HUD, 18 U.S.C. § 1012 (misdemeanor)
Frank Allen Els	E. D. Wash.	1976	Possession of an unregistered firearm, 26 U.S.C. § 5861(d)
Arthur Neil Evans	N. D. Calif.	1954	Protecting and assisting a deserter from the U.S. Army, 18 U.S.C. § 1381
Elizabeth Marie Frederick (fka Elizabeth Sigmon)	D. So. Dak.	1987	Distribution and possession with intent to distribute cocaine, 21 U.S.C. § 841(a)(1)
Jackie Lynn Gano	N. D. Iowa	1976	Receiving money or benefits through transactions of federal credit institution with intent to defraud while officer or employee of institution, 18 U.S.C. § 1006
Daniel Clifton Gilmour, Jr.	D. So. Car.	1985	Importation of marijuana, 21 U.S.C. §§ 952(a), 960, 963, and 18 U.S.C. § 2
Michael Lee Gilmour	D. So. Car.	1985	Importation of marijuana, 21 U.S.C. §§ 952(a), 960, 963, and 18 U.S.C. § 2
Theodore Avram Goodman	S. D. Calif.	1981	Unauthorized sale of government property, 18 U.S.C. § 641
Michael Charles Jorgensen	D. N. Mex.	1981	Misprision of a felony, 18 U.S.C. § 4
Leonard Charles Kampf	E. D. Va.	1990	Conveyance of government property without authority, 18 U.S.C. § 641
Kenneth Marshall Knull	Navy general court-martial	1976	Disobeying a lawful general order, negligently suffering destruction of military property, negligently hazarding two Naval vessels, Articles 92, 108, and 110, UCMJ
Reza Arabian Maleki	D. No. Dak.	1984	Conspiracy to make false statements to INS; false statements to INS, and aiding and abetting the same, 18 U.S.C. §§ 2, 371, and 1001
William Ronald McGuire	E. D. N. Y.	1978	Income tax evasion, 26 U.S.C. § 7201
Freddie Meeks	Navy general court-martial	1944	Making a mutiny during wartime
Steven Dwayne Miller	E. D. Tex.	1985	Possession of counterfeit Federal Reserve notes with intent to sell or otherwise use same, 18 U.S.C. § 474
Jodie David Moreland	W. D. La.	1987	Conspiracy to possess with intent to distribute marijuana, 21 U.S.C. §§ 841(a)(1), 841(b)(6), and 846
Lloyd Robert Odell	E. D. Wash.	1983	Theft of government property, 18 U.S.C. § 641

John Richard Palubicki	E. D. Wis.	1988	Conspiracy to defraud the IRS; income tax evasion, 18 U.S.C. § 371 and 26 U.S.C. § 7201
Patricia Ann Palubicki	E. D. Wis.	1988	Conspiracy to defraud the IRS; income tax evasion, 18 U.S.C. § 371 and 26 U.S.C. § 7201
Mark Edwin Pixley	D. Oregon	1991	Aiding in the manufacture, by cultivation, of marijuana, 21 U.S.C. § 841(a)(1) and 18 U.S.C. § 2
Theodore Alfred Rhone	D. Dist. Col.	1987	Wire fraud and aiding and abetting same, 18 U.S.C. §§ 2 and 1343
Warren David Samet	S. D. Fla.	1968	Transporting, concealing, and facilitating the transportation of marijuana that was acquired without paying the tax imposed, 26 U.S.C. § 4744(a)(2)
Steven Elliott Skorman	N. D. Ga.	1972	Distributing lysergic acid diethylamide (LSD), 21 U.S.C. § 841(a)(1)
Ronald Marsh Smith	Army general court-martial	1977	Stealing mail matter, Article 134, UCMJ
Richard Beauchamp Steele	S. D. Tex.	1989	Conspiracy to eliminate competition by fixing prices in interstate commerce, 15 U.S.C. § 1
Christine Ann Summerbell (fka Christine Ann McKeown)	W. D. Wis.	1984	Theft of mail by postal employee, 18 U.S.C. § 1709
Robert A. Suvino	W. D. Ark.	1988	Conspiracy to commit mail fraud and mail fraud, 18 U.S.C. §§ 371 and 1341
Daniel Larry Thomas, Jr.	N. D. Ohio	1987	Illegal use of a communication facility to distribute cocaine, 21 U.S.C. § 843
Howard Edwin Walraven	W. D. Ark.	1968	Theft from an interstate shipment, 18 U.S.C. § 659
Martin Harry Wesenberg	E. D. Wis.	1964	Willfully failing to pay the special occupational tax on wagering, and aiding and abetting the same, 26 U.S.C. § 7203 and 18 U.S.C. § 2 (misdemeanor)
Virgil Edwin West	N. D. Okla.	1982	Mail fraud, 18 U.S.C. §§ 2 and 1341

February 19, 2000			
NAME	DISTRICT	SENTENCED	OFFENSE
Preston Theodore King	1. M.D. Ga.	1. 1961	Failure to appear for physical examination; failure to appear for induction into the Armed Forces, 50 U.S.C. App. § 46
	2. M.D. Ga.	2. 1962 (indicted)	Bail jumping, 18 U.S.C. § 3146

March 15, 2000

NAME	DISTRICT	SENTENCED	OFFENSE
Gregory Leon Crosby	D. Maine	1987	Theft by postal employee, 18 U.S.C. § 1709
Everett Gale Dague	N. D. Iowa	1982	Conspiracy to obstruct commerce by extortion, extortion, demanding or receiving illegal payments on behalf of a labor union, and demanding or accepting illegal unloading fees from a motor vehicle driver, 18 U.S.C. §§ 2 and 1951, 29 U.S.C. §§186(b)(1) and (2)
Terry Stephen Duller	W. D. Wis.	1990	Engaging in illegal gambling business, 18 U.S.C. § 1955; failure to pay excise tax, 26 U.S.C. § 7262
Richard George Frye	D. Maine	1973	Knowingly shipping and transporting a firearm in interstate commerce, having been convicted of a felony, 18 U.S.C. §§ 922(g) and 924
Edgar Allen Gregory, Jr.	S. D. Ala.	1986	Conspiracy to willfully misapply bank funds, make false statements to a bank, and commit wire fraud; misapplication of bank funds by person connected with a bank, 18 U.S.C. §§ 371, 656, and 2
Vonna Jo Gregory	S. D. Ala.	1986	Conspiracy to willfully misapply bank funds, make false statements to a bank, and commit wire fraud; misapplication of bank funds by person connected with a bank, 18 U.S.C. §§ 371, 656, and 2
Carl David Hamilton	E. D. Ark.	1986	Bank fraud, and conspiracy to commit wire and bank fraud, 18 U.S.C. §§ 1343 and 371
Charles Edward Kirschner	D. Alaska	1993	Theft of bank property, 18 U.S.C. § 2113(b)
Charles Douglas Megla	W. D. Ky.	1980	Mail fraud, 18 U.S.C. §§ 1341 and 2
Owen Neil Nordine	D. Ariz.	1963	Interstate transportation of a stolen motor vehicle, 18 U.S.C. § 2312
William Thomas Rohring	D. Minn.	1986	Forgery of U.S. Treasury check, 18 U.S.C. § 510
Lawrence David Share	S. D. Calif.	1975	Conspiracy to commit securities fraud, sale of unregistered securities, and the use of manipulative devices in connection with the sale of securities, 18 U.S.C. §§ 371 and 2, and 15 U.S.C. §§ 77e(a), 77q(a), 77x, 78ff, and 78j(b)
Wayne Cletus Steinkamp	N. D. Iowa	1988	Conspiracy in restraint of trade in interstate commerce, 15 U.S.C. § 1
Peter John Thomas	D. Del.	1978	Conspiracy to possess cocaine with intent to distribute, 21 U.S.C. § 846
Heather Elizabeth Wilson (fka Heather Elizabeth	E. D. Okla.	1993	Use of telephone to facilitate commission of drug-trafficking felony, 21 U.S.C. § 843(b)

Calvin)			
Donna Marie Yellow Owl (fka Donna Marie Coursey)	D. Montana	1988	False statements, 18 U.S.C. § 1001

July 7, 2000			
NAME	DISTRICT	SENTENCED	OFFENSE
Carl Stanley Gilbreath	N. D. Ga.	1971	Interstate transportation of a stolen motor vehicle, 18 U.S.C. § 2312
Claudette Dean Goodson (fka Claudette Goodson Findeisen)	E. D. No. Car.	1986	Aiding and abetting embezzlement of government funds, 18 U.S.C. §§ 641 and 2
Dane Robert Hessling	S. D. Ohio	1987	Conspiracy to distribute and possess with intent to distribute cocaine, 21 U.S.C. § 846, and distribution and possession with intent to distribute cocaine, 21 U.S.C. § 841(a)(1)
Elwood Dwight Hopkins	D. New Jersey	1962	1. Theft of government property, 18 U.S.C. § 641 2. Mutilation of coins, 18 U.S.C. § 331
Thomas Vernon Jones	D. Wyo.	1989	Filing a false tax return 26 U.S.C. § 7206(1)
Madison Dow Kimball, Jr.	W. D. Ark.	1983	Bank robbery, 18 U.S.C. § 2113(a)
Cynthia Lou LeBlanc (fka Cynthia Lou Gallagher)	N. D. Tex.	1978	Conspiracy to distribute and possess methaqualone, 21 U.S.C. § 846
Peter Thomas Lipps	C. D. Calif.	1981	Possession of counterfeit government obligation, 18 U.S.C. § 472
John Carroll Michiaels	N. D. Ind.	1989	Purloining and converting property of the United States Environmental Protection Agency, and aiding and abetting therein, 18 U.S.C. §§ 641 and 2
Richard Edwin Sacchi	M. D. Fla.	1989	Conspiracy to possess cocaine with intent to distribute, 21 U.S.C. §§ 841(a)(1) and 846
Horace Carroll Smith	D. So. Car.	1992	Conspiracy to violate the federal securities laws, 18 U.S.C. §§ 371 and 2
Tammy Lawan	E. D. Okla.	1991	Misprision of a felony, 18 U.S.C. § 4

Tallant			
Carl Dennis Waren	W. D. Ark.	1980	Interstate transportation of stolen motor vehicles, 18 U.S.C. § 2314
Robert Alexander Warr	D. So. Car.	1982	False statements, 18 U.S.C. §§ 1001 and 2
James H. Wetzel, Jr.	E. D. La.	1981	Conspiracy to distribute cocaine, 18 U.S.C. § 371, and 21 U.S.C. § 841(a)(1)
Diane Mae Zeman (aka Diane Mae Moseman)	E. D. N. Y.	1981	Use of a telephone to facilitate importation of hashish oil, 21 U.S.C. § 843(b)

October 20, 2000			
NAME	DISTRICT	SENTENCED	OFFENSE
William Oshel Casto, III	E. D. Wis.	1984	Embezzlement by a bank employee, 18 U.S.C. § 656
Donald Demerest Hall	D. Del	1974	Misapplication of bank funds by an employee, 18 U.S.C. § 656
Cheryl Ada Elizabeth Little	S. D. Fla.	1978	Conspiracy with intent to distribute a controlled substance, 21 U.S.C. §§ 846 and 841(a)(1)
Joe Clint McMillan	M. D. No. Car.	1992	Conspiracy to violate the Sherman Antitrust Act, 15 U.S.C. § 1
Jeralyn Kay Rust	D. Minn.	1990	Wire fraud, 18 U.S.C. §§ 1343 and 2
Jane Marie Schoffstall	S. D. Calif.	1989	Possession with intent to distribute a controlled substance (methamphetamine), 21 U.S.C. § 841(a)(1)
William Calvin Smith, Jr.	E. D. Pa.	1970	Interstate transportation of a stolen motor vehicle, 18 U.S.C. § 2312

November 21, 2000			
NAME	DISTRICT	SENTENCED	OFFENSE
Glen David Curry	S. D. Ala.	1982	Conspiracy to distribute and possess with intent to distribute cocaine, distributing and possessing with intent to distribute cocaine, and using a telephone to facilitate distribution of cocaine, 21 U.S.C. §§ 841(a)(1), 843(b), and 846
Dave Meyer Hartson, III	E. D. La.	1993	Mail fraud, 18 U.S.C. §§ 1341 and 2
Carl Edward Karstetter	M. D. Pa.	1992	Conversion of government property, 18 U.S.C. § 641
Donald Spencer	S. D. Tex.	1991	False statements to a government agency, 18 U.S.C. § 1001

Lewis			
Walter Sidney Orlinsky	D. Md.	1982	Extortion under color of official right, 18 U.S.C. § 1951
Howard Charles Petersen	D. Neb.	1971	Embezzlement by a bank employee and making false entries in a bank's records, 18 U.S.C. §§ 656 and 1005
John Laurence Silvi	D. New Jersey	1992	Conspiracy to make unlawful payments to a union official, 18 U.S.C. § 371, 29 U.S.C. § 186
Laurence John Silvi, II	D. New Jersey	1992	Conspiracy to bribe a union official, 18 U.S.C. § 371, 29 U.S.C. § 186
John Donald Vodde	N. D. Ind.	1989	Possession and distribution of cocaine, and aiding and abetting, 21 U.S.C. § 841(a)(1) and 18 U.S.C. § 2
Melinda Kay Stewart Vodde	N. D. Ind.	1989	Distribution of cocaine, and aiding and abetting, 21 U.S.C. § 841(a)(1) and 18 U.S.C. § 2
Philip Donald Winn	D. Dist. Col.	1994	Conspiracy to give illegal gratuities, 18 U.S.C. § 371

December 22, 2000			
NAME	DISTRICT	SENTENCED	OFFENSE
Jimmy Lee Allen	W. D. Ark.	1990	False statements to agency of United States, 15 U.S.C. § 714m(a)
Virgil Lamoin Baker	E. D. (now S. D.) Ill.	1959	Violation of the Military Training and Service Act, 50 U.S.C. App. § 462
Garran Dee Barker	E. D. Ark	1986	Conspiracy to commit bank and wire fraud, 18 U.S.C. § 371
Nancy M. Baxter	W. D. Va.	1990	Tax evasion and filing a false amended tax return; 26 U.S.C. §§ 7201 and 7206(1)
Charles N. Besser	N. D. Ill	1985	Mail fraud, 18 U.S.C. § 1341
Harlan Richard Billings	D. Maine	1985	Conspiracy to possess with intent to distribute in excess of 1,000 pounds of marijuana, 21 U.S.C. § 846
Edward Raymond Birdseye	E. D. Calif.	1992	Unlawful use of a communication facility, 21 U.S.C. § 843(b)
Roscoe Crosby Blunt, Jr.	Army court-martial	1945	Fraternization, Article of War 96
Charles Edward Boggs	E. D. Ark.	1977	Receiving a stolen motor vehicle which was part of interstate commerce, 18 U.S.C. § 2313
Terry Coy Bonner	N. D. W. Va.	1986	Possession of an illegally made destructive device, 26 U.S.C. § 5861(c)
Alfred Whitney Brown, III	E. D. La.	1992	Illegal sale of wildlife by allowing hunting over a baited field, 16 U.S.C. §§ 3372(a)(1), 3372(c)(1)(A), and 3373(d)(1)(B), and 18 U.S.C. §

			2
William Robert Carpenter	N. D. Calif.	1991	Possession of marijuana with intent to distribute, 21 U.S.C. § 841(a)(1)
Philip Vito DiGirolamo	N. D. Calif.	1984	Conspiracy to import marijuana, 21 U.S.C. § 963; willfully subscribing to a false tax return, 26 U.S.C. § 7206(1)
Peter Welling Dionis	N. D. N. Y.	1976	Conspiracy, importation, and possession with intent to distribute hashish, 21 U.S.C. §§ 841(a)(1), 952(a), and 963, and 18 U.S.C. § 2
Darrin Dean Dorn	S. D. Iowa	1981	Conspiracy to damage property by means and use of an explosive, 18 U.S.C. § 371
Peter Bailey Gimbel	S. D. N. Y.	1991	Conspiracy to distribute cocaine, 21 U.S.C. § 846
Philip Joseph Grandmaison	D. New Hamp.	1996	Mail fraud, 18 U.S.C. §§ 1341 and 1346
Joe Robert Grist	W. D. Tex.	1990	Misapplication of funds by a bank employee, 18 U.S.C. § 656
LeRoy Kenneth Hartung, Jr.	D. Nev.	1986	Interception of wire communications, 18 U.S.C. § 2511(1)(a)
Joseph Riddick Hendrick, III	W. D. No. Car.	1997	Mail fraud, 18 U.S.C. § 1341
Judd Blair Hirschberg	N. D. Ill.	1991	Mail fraud, 18 U.S.C. § 1341
Robert Quinn Houston	S. D. Miss.	1986	Conspiracy to obstruct commerce by extortion, 18 U.S.C. § 1951(a)
Martin Joseph Hughes	N. D. Ohio	1987	Aiding and abetting the falsification of union records, aiding and assisting in the submission of false tax records, making false statements to a government agency, 29 U.S.C. § 439(c) and 18 U.S.C. § 2, 26 U.S.C. § 7204, 18 U.S.C. § 1001 (as modified)
Jere Wayne Johnson	W. D. Okla.	1982	Conspiracy to defraud the United States and Garfield County, Oklahoma, while serving as a county commissioner, 18 U.S.C. § 371
Michael Thomas Johnson	S. D. Miss.	1987	Filing false tax returns, 26 U.S.C. § 7206(1)
Daniel Wayne Keys	S. D. Tex.	1977	Possession with intent to distribute marijuana, 21 U.S.C. § 841(a)(1)
Larry Ray Killough	E. D. Ark.	1985	Unlawful distribution of prescription drugs, 21 U.S.C. § 841(a)(1)
Jack Kligman	E. D. Pa.	1985	Conspiracy and mail fraud, 18 U.S.C. §§ 371 and 1341
Hector Osvaldo Labagnara	D. New Jersey	1976	Conspiracy to transport stolen motor vehicles in interstate commerce, to receive and sell stolen motor vehicles, to transport false vehicle registrations in interstate commerce, and to receive and dispose of false vehicle registrations; receipt

				and sale of stolen motor vehicles; 18 U.S.C. §§ 371 and 2313
Moses Jubilee Lestz (fka Michael Eugene Lestz)	W. D. Ark.	1982		Forgery of United States savings bond, 18 U.S.C. § 495
Leon Lee Liebscher	W. D. Okla.	1982		Conspiracy to defraud the United States (tax evasion), 18 U.S.C. § 371
Pierluigi Mancini	N. D. Ga.	1985		Possession of cocaine with intent to distribute, 21 U.S.C. § 841(a)
John Ross McCown, Jr.	D. Neb.	1992		Structuring of transactions to evade reporting requirements, 31 U.S.C. §§ 5324(3) and 5322(b) and 18 U.S.C. § 2
Edward Francis McKenna, III	S. D. Miss.	1993		Possession with intent to distribute anabolic steroids, 21 U.S.C. § 333(e)(1)
Andrew Kirkpatrick Mearns, III	D. Del.	1978		Conspiracy to distribute and possess with intent to distribute cocaine, 21 U.S.C. §§ 846 and 841
Ralph Eugene Meczyk	N. D. Ill.	1987		Filing false partnership and individual federal income tax returns, and aiding and abetting therein, 26 U.S.C. § 7206(1) and 18 U.S.C. § 2
Philip James Morin	W. D. Tex.	1984		Distribution of cocaine; 21 U.S.C. § 841(a)(1)
Thomas Edward Nash, Jr.	W. D. No. Car.	1988		Conspiracy to restrain interstate trade and commerce, 15 U.S.C. § 1
Roger Lee Nelson	D. Neb.	1981		Aiding and abetting mail fraud, 18 U.S.C. §§ 1341 and 2
Jose Rene Pineda-Martinez	1. S. D. Tex.	1. 1983		Entering U.S. without inspection (misdemeanor), 8 U.S.C. § 1325
	2. S. D. Tex.	2. 1983		Transporting an illegal alien within the U.S., 8 U.S.C. § 1324(a)(2)
	3. S. D. Tex.	3. 1984		Transporting an illegal alien within the U.S., 8 U.S.C. § 1324(a)(2)
John Russell Raup	Air Force general court-martial	1984		Larceny of government property and wrongful possession of marijuana; U.C.M.J. Articles 121 and 134
James William Rogers	D. So. Car.	1983 (as modified)		Conspiracy to commit racketeering, 18 U.S.C. § 1962(d)
George Wisham Roper, II	E. D. Va.	1974		Conspiracy to bribe public officials and to defraud the United States government, 18 U.S.C. § 371
Daniel Rostenkowski	D. Dist. Col.	1996		Mail fraud (two counts), 18 U.S.C. §§ 1341 and 1346

Dean Raymond Rush	W. D. Tex.	1993	False statements on a loan application, 18 U.S.C. § 1014
Archibald R. Schaffer, III	D. Dist. Col.	2000	Violation of the Meat Inspection Act, 21 U.S.C. § 622
Anthony Andrew Schmidt	D. Kan.	1985	Conspiracy to possess and distribute cocaine, 21 U.S.C. §§ 841(a)(1) and 846
Stanley Sirote	E. D. N. Y.	1974	Bribery of a public official, 18 U.S.C. § 201(f)
Dent Elwood Snider, Jr.	D. Colo.	1981	Use of a telephone to facilitate the distribution of cocaine, 21 U.S.C. § 843(b)
James Lawrence Swisher	M. D. No. Car.	1977	Obstruction of a criminal investigation, 18 U.S.C. § 1510
Larry Kalvy Thompson	N. D. Tex.	1988	Aiding and abetting misapplication of bank funds, misprision of a felony, 18 U.S.C. §§ 2, 4, and 657
Stephanie Marie Vetter	D. New Mex.	1979	Possession with intent to distribute methamphetamine, 21 U.S.C. § 841(a)(1)
Danny Ray Walker	E. D. Ark.	1975	Interstate transportation of stolen property, 18 U.S.C. § 2316
Thomas Andrew Warren	S. D. Fla.	1975	Conspiracy to import marijuana, 21 U.S.C. § 963
Michael Lynn Weatherford	E. D. No. Car.	1986	Aiding and abetting interstate travel in aid of racketeering, 18 U.S.C. §§ 1952(a) and 2
Jack Weinstein	D. Nev.	1975	Conspiracy and interstate transportation of stolen property, 18 U.S.C. §§ 371, 2314, and 2
Robert Owen Wilson	M. D. Tenn.	1980	Mail fraud, 18 U.S.C. § 1341
Charles Elvin Witherspoon	E. D. Tex.	1977	Embezzlement of bank funds, 18 U.S.C. § 656
Charles Z. Yonce, Jr.	D. So. Car.	1988	Conspiracy to possess with intent to distribute cocaine and aiding and abetting therein, 21 U.S.C. §§ 841(a)(1), 846, and 841(b)(1)(B), and 18 U.S.C. § 2

January 20, 2001
(Clinton's last day in office)

NAME	DISTRICT	SENTENCED	OFFENSE
Verla Jean Allen	W. D. Ark.	1990	False statements to agency of United States, 15 U.S.C. § 714m(a)
Bernice Ruth Altschul	D. Ariz.	1992	Conspiracy to commit money laundering, 18 U.S.C. § 371
Nicholas M. Altiere	S. D. Fla.	1983	Importation of cocaine, 21 U.S.C. §§ 952(a)(1) and 960(a)(1)
Joe Anderson, Jr.	S. D. Ala.	1988	Income tax evasion, 26 U.S.C. § 7201
William Sterling Anderson	D. So. Car.	1987	Conspiracy to defraud a federally insured financial institution, false statements to a federally insured financial institution, wire fraud, 18 U.S.C. §§ 2, 371, 1014, and 1343
Mansour T. Azizkhani	W. D. Okla.	1984	Conspiracy and making false statements in bank loan applications, 18 U.S.C. §§ 371, 1014
Cleveland Victor Babin, Jr.	W. D. Okla.	1987	Conspiracy to commit offense against the United States by utilizing the U.S. mail in furtherance of a scheme to defraud, 18 U.S.C. § 371
Chris Harmon Bagley	W. D. Okla.	1989	Conspiracy to possess with intent to distribute cocaine, 21 U.S.C. § 846
Scott Lynn Bane	C. D. Ill.	1984	Unlawful distribution of marijuana, 21 U.S.C. § 841(a)(1) and 18 U.S.C. § 2
Thomas Cleveland Barber	M. D. Fla.	1977	Issuing worthless checks, 18 U.S.C. §§ 7 and 13
Peggy Ann Bargon	C. D. Ill.	1995	Violation of Lacey Act, violation of Bald Eagle Protection Act, 16 U.S.C. §§ 3372(a)(1), 3373(d)(2), and 668(a); 18 U.S.C. § 2
Tansukhlal Bhatka	W. D. Ark.	1991	Filing fraudulent income tax returns, 26 U.S.C. § 7201
David Roscoe Blampied	D. Idaho	1979	Conspiracy to distribute cocaine, 26 U.S.C. § 846
William Arthur Borders, Jr.	N. D. Ga.	1982	Conspiracy to corruptly solicit and accept money in return for influencing the official acts of a federal district court judge, and to defraud the United States in connection with the performance of lawful government functions; corruptly influencing, obstructing, impeding, and endeavoring to influence, obstruct, and impede the due administration of justice, and aiding and abetting therein; traveling interstate with intent to commit bribery, 18 U.S.C. §§ 371, 1503, 2, and 1952
Arthur David Borel	E. D. Ark.	1991	Odometer rollback, 15 U.S.C. § 1984
Douglas Charles Borel	E. D. Ark.	1991	Odometer rollback, 15 U.S.C. § 1984
George	E. D. Tex.	1989	Making a false statement or report to a

Thomas Brabham			federally insured bank, 18 U.S.C. § 1014
Almon Glenn Braswell	1. N. D. Ga.	1. 1983	1. Mail fraud, 18 U.S.C. § 1341
	2. N. D. Ga.	2. 1983	2. Perjury, 18 U.S.C. § 1623
	3. N. D. Ga.	3. 1983	3. Filing false income tax return, 26 U.S.C. § 7206(1)
Leonard Browder	D. So. Car.	1990	Illegal dispensing of controlled substance and Medicaid fraud, 21 U.S.C. §§ 827(a)(3), 843(a)(3), 843(a)(4)(A), and 843(c); 18 U.S.C. §§ 1341 and 2
David Steven Brown	S. D. N. Y.	1987	Securities fraud and mail fraud, 15 U.S.C. §§ 78j(b) and 78ff; 18 U.S.C. §§ 1341 and 2; 17 C.F.R. §240.106-5
Delores Caroylene Burleson	E. D. Okla.	1978	Possession of marijuana, 21 U.S.C. § 844(a)
John H. Bustamante	N. D. Ohio	1993	Wire fraud, 18 U.S.C. § 1343
Mary Louise Campbell	N. D. Miss.	1988	Aiding and abetting the unauthorized use and transfer of food stamps, 18 U.S.C. § 2 and 7 U.S.C. § 2024(b)
Eloida Candelaria	D. New Mex.	1992	False information in registering to vote, 42 U.S.C. § 1973i(c)
Dennis Sobrevinas Capili	E. D. Calif.	1990	Filing false statements in alien registration, 8 U.S.C. § 1306(c)
Donna Denise Chambers	E. D. Wis.	1986	Conspiracy to possess with intent to distribute and to distribute cocaine, possession with intent to distribute cocaine, use of a telephone to facilitate cocaine conspiracy, 21 U.S.C. §§ 846, 841(a)(1), and 843(b)
Douglas Eugene Chapman	E. D. Ark.	1993	Bank fraud, 18 U.S.C. § 1344
Ronald Keith Chapman	E. D. Ark.	1993	Bank fraud, 18 U.S.C. § 1344
Francisco Larios Chavez	S. D. Calif.	1986	Aiding and abetting illegal entry of aliens, 8 U.S.C. § 1325 and 18 U.S.C. § 2
Henry G. Cisneros	D. Dist. Col.	1999	False statement (misdemeanor), 18 U.S.C. § 1018
Roger Clinton	1. W. D. Ark.	1. 1985	1. Conspiracy to distribute cocaine, 21 U.S.C. § 846
	2. W.D. Ark.	2. 1985	2. Distribution of cocaine, 21 U.S.C. § 841(a)(1)
Stuart Harris Cohn	S. D. N. Y.	1983	Illegal sale of commodity options, 7 U.S.C. §§ 6c(c) and 13(b), and 18 U.S.C. § 2
David M. Cooper	N. D. Ohio	1992	Conspiracy to defraud the government, 18 U.S.C. § 371
Ernest Harley Cox, Jr.	E. D. Ark.	1991	Conspiracy to defraud a federally insured savings and loan, misapplication of bank funds,

			false statements, 18 U.S.C. §§ 371, 657, and 1014
John F. Cross, Jr.	E. D. Ark.	1995	Embezzlement, 18 U.S.C. § 656
Rickey Lee Cunningham	S. D. Tex.	1973	Possession with intent to distribute marijuana, 21 U.S.C. § 841(a)(1)
Richard Anthony De Labio	D. Md.	1977	Mail fraud, aiding and abetting, 18 U.S.C. §§ 1341 and 2
John Deutch	D. Dist. Col.	2001 information	Offenses charged in January 19, 2001, information
Richard Douglas	N. D. Calif.	1998	False statements to a government agent, 18 U.S.C. § 1001
Edward Reynolds Downe, Jr.	S. D. N. Y.	1993	Conspiracy to commit wire fraud and to subscribe to false income tax returns, securities fraud, 18 U.S.C. § 371 and 15 U.S.C. §§ 78p and 78ff
Marvin Dean Dudley	D. Neb.	1992	False statements, 18 U.S.C. § 1014
Larry Lee Duncan	W. D. Okla.	1992	Altering an automobile odometer, 15 U.S.C. § 1984
Robert Clinton Fain	E. D. Ark.	1982	Aiding and assisting in the preparation and filing of a false corporate tax return, 26 U.S.C. § 7206(2)
Marcos Arcenio Fernandez	S. D. Fla.	1980	Conspiracy to possess with intent to distribute marijuana, 21 U.S.C. § 846
Alvarez Ferrouillet	1. E. D. La.	1. 1997	Interstate transportation of stolen property, 18 U.S.C. § 2314; money laundering, 18 U.S.C. § 1956(a)(1) (b)(i); engaging in a monetary transaction with criminally derived property, 18 U.S.C. § 1957; false statements to government agents, 18 U.S.C. § 1001
	2. N. D. Miss.	2. 1997	Conspiracy to make false statements to a financial institution, 18 U.S.C. §§ 371 and 1014
William Denis Fugazy	S. D. N. Y.	1997	Perjury in a bankruptcy proceeding, 18 U.S.C. § 152
Lloyd Reid George	E. D. Ark.	1997	Aiding and abetting mail fraud, 18 U.S.C. §§ 1341 and 2
Louis Goldstein	N. D. Ill.	1985	Possession of goods stolen from interstate shipment, 18 U.S.C. § 659
Rubye Lee Gordon	M. D. Ga.	1974	Forgery of U.S. Treasury checks, 18 U.S.C. § 495
Pincus Green	S. D. N. Y.	1984 superseding indictment	Wire fraud, mail fraud, racketeering, racketeering conspiracy, criminal forfeiture, income tax evasion, and trading with Iran in violation of trade embargo, 18 U.S.C. §§ 1343, 1341, 1962(c), 1962(d), 1963, and 2; 26 U.S.C. § 7201, 50 U.S.C. § 1705, and 31 C.F.R. §§ 535.206(a)(4), 535.208 and 535.701
Robert Ivey	C. D. Ill.	1986	Conspiracy to distribute marijuana, possession

Hamner			of marijuana with intent to distribute, 21 U.S.C. §§ 846 and 841(a)(1)
Samuel Price Handley	W. D. Ky.	1963	Conspiracy to steal government property, 18 U.S.C. § 371
Woodie Randolph Handley	W. D. Ky.	1963	Conspiracy to steal government property, 18 U.S.C. § 371
Jay Houston Harmon	1. E. D. Ark.	1. 1982	Conspiracy to import marijuana, conspiracy to possess marijuana with intent to distribute, importation of marijuana, possession of marijuana with intent to distribute, 21 U.S.C. §§ 963, 846, 952, and 841(a)
	2. M. D. Ga.	2. 1986	Conspiracy to import cocaine, 21 U.S.C. §§ 952, 960, and 963
John J. Hemmingson	E. D. La.	1997	Interstate transportation of stolen property, 18 U.S.C. § 2314; money laundering, 18 U.S.C. § 1956(a)(1)(b)(i); engaging in a monetary transaction with criminally derived property, 18 U.S.C. § 1957
David S. Herdlinger	W. D. Ark.	1986	Mail fraud, 18 U.S.C. § 1341
Debi Rae Huckleberry, (fka Debi Rae VanDenakker)	D. Utah	1986	Distribution of methamphetamine, 21 U.S.C. § 841(a)(1)
Donald Ray James	W. D. Tenn.	1983	Mail fraud, wire fraud, and false statements to a bank to influence credit approval, 18 U.S.C. §§ 1341, 1343, and 1014
Stanley Pruet Jobe	W. D. Tex.	1994	Conspiracy to commit bank fraud, bank fraud, 18 U.S.C. §§ 371, 1005, 1014, and 1344
Ruben H. Johnson	W. D. Tex.	1989	Theft and misapplication of bank funds by a bank officer or director (13 counts), 18 U.S.C. § 656
Linda Jones, (fka Linda D. Medlar)	N. D. Tex.	1998	Conspiracy to commit bank fraud, to make a false statement to a bank, to launder monetary instruments, and to engage in monetary transactions in property derived from specific unlawful activity; aiding and abetting bank fraud; aiding and abetting false statements to a bank; aiding and abetting laundering monetary instruments; aiding and abetting engaging in monetary transactions in property derived from specific unlawful activity; obstruction of justice; falsifying, concealing and covering up a material fact by trick, scheme, or device; making a false statement; 18 U.S.C. §§ 2, 371, 1001, 1014, 1344(1) and (2), 1503, 1956(a)(1)(A)(i) and (B)(i), and 1957
James Howard Lake	D. Dist. Col.	1998	Illegal corporate campaign contributions (two counts), wire fraud, 2 U.S.C. §§ 437g(d)(1)(A), 441b(a), and 441f, and 18 U.S.C. §§ 2, 1343, and 1346

June Louise Lewis	N. D. Ohio	1991	Embezzlement by a bank employee, 18 U.S.C. § 656
Salim Bonnor Lewis	S. D. N. Y.	1989	Securities fraud, record keeping violations, margin violations, 15 U.S.C. §§ 78ff, 78g(a), 78g(f), and 78j(b), and 18 U.S.C. § 2
John Leighton Lodwick	W. D. Mo.	1968	Income tax evasion, 26 U.S.C. § 7201
Hildebrando Lopez	S. D. Tex.	1981	Distribution of cocaine, 21 U.S.C. § 841(a)(1)
Jose Julio Luaces, Jr.	S. D. Fla.	1989	Possession of an unregistered firearm, 26 U.S.C. §§ 5861(d) and 5871
James Timothy Maness	W. D. Tenn.	1985	Conspiracy to distribute Valium, 21 U.S.C. §§ 846 and 841(a)(1)
James Lowell Manning	E. D. Ark.	1982	Aiding and assisting in the preparation of a false corporate income tax return, 26 U.S.C. § 7206(2)
John Robert Martin	N. D. Fla.	1987	Income tax evasion, 26 U.S.C. § 7201
Frank Ayala Martinez	W. D. Tex.	1989	Conspiracy to supply false documents to the Immigration and Naturalization Service, 18 U.S.C. § 371
Silvia Leticia Beltran Martinez	W. D. Tex.	1989	Conspiracy to supply false documents to the Immigration and Naturalization Service, 18 U.S.C. § 371
John Francis McCormick	D. Mass.	1988	Racketeering, racketeering conspiracy, aiding and abetting Hobbjay houston harmons Act extortion (five counts), 18 U.S.C. §§ 1962(c) and (d), 1951, and 2
Susan H. McDougal	E. D. Ark.	1996	Mail fraud, 18 U.S.C. § 1341; aiding and abetting in misapplication of Small Business Investment Corporation funds, 18 U.S.C. §§ 657 and 2; aiding and abetting in making false entries, 18 U.S.C. §§ 1006 and 2; aiding and abetting in making false statements, 18 U.S.C. §§ 1014 and 2
Howard Lawrence Mechanic, (aka Gary Robert Tredway)	1. E. D. Mo.	1. 1970	Violating the Civil Disobedience Act of 1968, 18 U.S.C. § 213(a)
	2. D. Ariz.	2. 2000	Failure to appear, 18 U.S.C. § 3150
	3. D. Ariz.	3. 2000	Making a false statement in acquiring a passport, 18 U.S.C. § 1542
Brook K. Mitchell, Sr.	D. Dist. Col.	1999	Conspiracy to illegally obtain USDA subsidy payments, false statements to USDA (two counts), false entries on USDA forms, 15 U.S.C. §§ 741m(d), 714m(a), and 714m(b)(ii); 18 U.S.C. § 2
Charles Wilfred Morgan, III	W. D. Ark.	1984	Conspiracy to distribute cocaine, 18 U.S.C. § 371
Samuel Loring	D. Md.	1985	Willful transmission of defense information, unauthorized possession and retention of

Morison			defense information, theft of government property, 18 U.S.C. §§ 641, 793(d), and 793(e)
Richard Anthony Nazzaro	D. Mass.	1988	Perjury and conspiracy to commit mail fraud, 18 U.S.C. §§ 371 and 1623
Charlene Ann Nosenko	N. D. Ill.	1990	Conspiracy to defraud the United States, and influencing or injuring an officer or juror generally, 18 U.S.C. §§ 371 and 1503
Vernon Raymond Obermeier	S. D. Ill.	1989	Conspiracy to distribute cocaine, distribution of cocaine, and using a communications facility to facilitate distribution of cocaine, 21 U.S.C. §§ 846, 841(a)(1), and 843(b)
Miguelina Ogalde	D. Puerto Rico	1981	Conspiracy to import cocaine, 21 U.S.C. §§ 952(a) and 963
David C. Owen	D. Kans.	1993	Filing a false tax return, 26 U.S.C. § 7206(1)
Robert William Palmer	E. D. Ark.	1995	Conspiracy to make false statements, 18 U.S.C. § 371
Kelli Anne Perhosky (fka Kelli Anne Flynn)	W. D. Pa.	1989	Conspiracy to commit mail fraud, 18 U.S.C. § 371
Richard H. Pezzopane	N. D. Ill.	1988	Conspiracy to commit racketeering, mail fraud, 18 U.S.C. §§ 1962(d) and 1341
Orville Rex Phillips	W. D. Tex.	1991	Unlawful structuring of a financial transaction, 31 U.S.C. § 5324
Vinson Stewart Poling, Jr.	D. Md.	1980	Making a false bank entry, and aiding and abetting, 18 U.S.C. §§ 1005 and 2
Normal Lyle Prouse	D. Minn.	1990	Operating or directing the operation of a common carrier while under the influence of alcohol, 18 U.S.C. § 342
Willie H. H. Pruitt, Jr.	U.S. Air Force special court-martial	1954	Absent without official leave, UCMJ
Danny Martin Pursley, Sr.	M. D. Tenn.	1991	Aiding and abetting the conduct of an illegal gambling business, and obstruction of state laws to facilitate illegal gambling, 18 U.S.C. §§ 1511, 1955, and 2
Charles D. Ravenel	D. So. Car.	1996	Conspiring to defraud the United States, 18 U.S.C. § 371
William Clyde Ray	W. D. Okla.	1989	Fraud using the telephone, 18 U.S.C. § 1343
Alfredo Luna Regalado	S. D. Tex.	1987	Failure to report the transportation of currency in excess of $10,000 into the United States, 31 U.S.C. § 5316(a)(1)(B)
Ildefonso Reynes Ricafort	Veterans Administration Compensation	1987	Submission of false claims to Veterans Administration, 38 U.S.C. § 3503(a), now codified at 38 U.S.C. § 6103(a)

	and Pension Service		
Marc Rich	S. D. N. Y.	1984 superseding indictment	Wire fraud, mail fraud, racketeering, racketeering conspiracy, criminal forfeiture, income tax evasion, and trading with Iran in violation of trade embargo, 18 U.S.C. §§ 1343, 1341, 1962(c), 1962(d), 1963, and 2; 26 U.S.C. § 7201, 50 U.S.C. § 1705, and 31 C.F.R. §§ 535.206(a)(4), 535.208 and 535.701
Howard Winfield Riddle	N. D. Tex.	1989	Violation of the Lacey Act (receipt of illegally imported animal skins), 18 U.S.C. § 545
Richard Wilson Riley, Jr.	D. So. Car.	1993	Conspiring to possess with intent to distribute and to distribute marijuana and cocaine, 21 U.S.C. § 846
Samuel Lee Robbins	W. D. Tex.	1990	Misprision of a felony, 18 U.S.C. § 4
Joel Gonzales Rodriguez	S. D. Tex.	1991	Theft of mail by a postal employee, 18 U.S.C. § 1709
Michael James Rogers	S. D. Tex.	1977	Conspiracy to possess with intent to distribute marijuana, 21 U.S.C. §§ 841(a)(1) and 846
Anna Louise Ross	N. D. Tex.	1988	Distribution of cocaine, 21 U.S.C. § 841(a)(1); 18 U.S.C. § 2
Gerald Glen Rust	E. D. Tex.	1991	False declarations before grand jury, 18 U.S.C. § 1623
Jerri Ann Rust	E. D. Tex.	1991	False declarations before grand jury, 18 U.S.C. § 1623
Bettye June Rutherford	D. New Mex.	1992	Possession of marijuana with intent to distribute, 21 U.S.C. §§ 841(a)(1) and (b)(1)(D)
Gregory Lee Sands	D. So. Dak.	1990	Conspiracy to distribute cocaine, 21 U.S.C. §§ 841 and 846
Adolph Schwimmer	S. D. Calif.	1950	Conspiracy to violate the Neutrality Act and export control laws, and conspiracy to export arms, ammunition, etc. to a foreign country, in violation of 18 U.S.C. §§ 88 (1946 ed.) and 371, 22 U.S.C. § 452, and 50 U.S.C. § 701
Albert A. Seretti, Jr.	D. Nev.	1983	Conspiracy and wire fraud, 18 U.S.C. §§ 2, 371, 1343
Patricia Campbell Hearst Shaw	N. D. Calif.	1976	Armed bank robbery and using a firearm during a felony, 18 U.S.C. §§ 2113(a) and (d) and 924(c)(1)
Dennis Joseph Smith	1. U.S. Army summary court-martial	1. 1951	1. Unauthorized absence
	2. U.S. Army summary court-martial	2. 1952	2. Failure to obey off limits instructions
	3. U.S. Army special court-martial	3. 1954	3. Unauthorized absence

Gerald Owen Smith	S. D. Miss.	1956	Armed bank robbery, 18 U.S.C. § 2113
Stephen A. Smith	E. D. Ark.	1996	Conspiracy to misapply Small Business Administration loans, 18 U.S.C. § 371
Jimmie Lee Speake	N. D. Tex.	1976	Conspiracy to possess and utter counterfeit $20 Federal Reserve notes, 18 U.S.C. § 371
Charles Bernard Stewart	M. D. Ga.	1986	Illegally destroying U.S. mail, 18 U.S.C. § 1703(a)
Marlena Francisca Stewart-Rollins	N. D. Ohio	1989	Conspiracy to distribute cocaine, 21 U.S.C. § 846
John Fife Symington, III	D. Ariz.	1996 indictment; 1997 superseding indictment	False statements to federally insured financial institutions, wire fraud, attempted extortion, and false statements in bankruptcy proceeding, 18 U.S.C. §§ 1014, 1343, 1951, 152, 2(a) and 2(b)
Richard Lee Tannehill	D. Colo.	1990	Conspiracy in restraint of trade, 15 U.S.C. § 1
Nicholas C. Tenaglia	E. D. Pa.	1985	Receipt of illegal payments under the Medicare Program, 42 U.S.C. § 1395nn(b)(1)(B)
Gary Allen Thomas	W. D. Tex.	1987	Theft of mail by postal employee, 18 U.S.C. § 1709
Larry Weldon Todd	W. D. Tex.	1983	Conspiracy to commit an offense against the United States in violation of the Lacey Act and the Airborne Hunting Act, 18 U.S.C. § 371; 16 U.S.C. §§ 3372(a)(1), 3373(d)(1)(B), and 742j-1
Olga C. Trevino	W. D. Tex.	1987	Misapplication by a bank employee, 18 U.S.C. § 656
Ignatious Vamvouklis	D. New. Hamp.	1991	Possession of cocaine, 21 U.S.C. § 844(a)
Patricia A. Van De Weerd	W. D. Wis.	1990	Theft by U.S. postal employee, 18 U.S.C. § 1711
Christopher V. Wade	E. D. Ark.	1995	Bank fraud and false statements on a loan application, 18 U.S.C. §§ 152 and 1014
Bill Wayne Warmath	W. D. Tenn.	1965	Obstruction of correspondence, 18 U.S.C. § 1720
Jack Kenneth Watson	D. Oregon	1985	Making false statements of material facts to the United States Forest Service, 18 U.S.C. § 1001
Donna Lynn Webb	N. D. Fla.	1989	False entry in savings and loan record by employee, 18 U.S.C. § 1006
Donald William Wells	M. D. No. Car.	1973	Possession of an unregistered firearm, 26 U.S.C. §§ 5861(d) and 5871
Robert H. Wendt	E. D. Mo.	1982	Conspiracy to effectuate the escape of a federal prisoner, 18 U.S.C. § 371
Jack L. Williams	D. Dist. Col.	1998	Making false statements to federal agents (two counts), 18 U.S.C. § 1001
Kevin Arthur	D. Neb.	1990	Conspiracy to distribute and possess with intent

Williams			to distribute crack cocaine, 21 U.S.C. § 846
Robert Michael Williams	E. D. Mich.	1981	Conspiracy to transport in foreign commerce securities obtained by fraud, 18 U.S.C. §§ 371 and 2314
Jimmie Lee Wilson	E. D. Ark.	1990	Converting property mortgaged or pledged to a farm credit agency, and converting public money to personal use, 18 U.S.C. §§ 641 and 658
Thelma Louise Wingate	M. D. Ga.	1991	Mail fraud, 18 U.S.C. §§ 1341 and 2
Mitchell Couey Wood	E. D. Ark.	1986	Conspiracy to possess and to distribute cocaine, 18 U.S.C. § 371 and 21 U.S.C. § 841(a)
Warren Stannard Wood	S. D. Calif.	1978	Conspiracy to defraud the United States by filing a false document with the Securities and Exchange Commission, 18 U.S.C. § 371; 15 U.S.C. §§ 78m. 78n, and 78ff
Dewey Worthey	E. D. Ark.	1988	Medicaid fraud, 42 U.S.C. § 1396
Rick Allen Yale	S. D. Ill.	1992	Bank fraud, 18 U.S.C. §§ 1344 and 2
Joseph A. Yasak	N. D. Ill.	1988	Knowingly making under oath a false declaration regarding a material fact before a Grand Jury, 18 U.S.C. § 1623
William Stanley Yingling	E. D. Ark.	1979	Receipt of a stolen motor vehicle, 18 U.S.C. § 2313
Philip David Young	W. D. La.	1992	Interstate transportation and sale of fish and wildlife, 16 U.S.C. §§ 3372(a)(2)(A) and 3373(d)(1)(B)

Appendix B

The Clinton Body Count

The following is a partial list of deaths of persons connected to Bill and Hillary in one way or another during his tenure as Governor of Arkansas and as President of the United States. No implication should be made that any of the below deaths were the result of any specific person's action and that the deaths were anything other than natural causes or as a result other than publicly determined. However, having dirt on the Clintons just doesn't seem to be a wise path if you want to live a long and healthy life. Read the list and judge for yourself.

JAMES MCDOUGAL-Clinton's convicted Whitewater partner died of an apparent heart attack, while in solitary confinement. McDougal was a key witness in Kenneth Starr's investigation.

MARY MAHONEY- A former White House intern was murdered July 6, 1997 at a Starbucks Coffee Shop in Georgetown. The murder happened during the pre-trial publicity surrounding the Paula Jones lawsuit; days after Newsweek's Mike Isikoff dropped hints that a former White House staffer was about to go public with her story of sexual harassment in the White House.

VINCENT FOSTER - Former White House counselor, and former colleague of Hillary Clinton at Little Rock's Rose law firm. Foster was found dead July 20, 1993 of a gunshot to the head, ruled a suicide.

RON BROWN - Secretary of Commerce and former DNC Chairman. It was reported that he died by impact in a plane crash. A pathologist close to the investigation reported to the Bob Grant Radio Show a "hole" in top of Brown's skull resembling a gunshot wound. At the time of his death Brown was being investigated, and spoke publicly of his willingness to cut a deal with prosecutors.

C. VICTOR RAISER II - Former National finance Co-Chairman, Clinton for President Campaign and son MONTGOMERY RAISER died in a private plane crash in Alaska, July 30th, 1992. Raiser was described as a "major player" in the Clinton organization by Dee Dee Meyers.

PAUL TULLEY - Democrat National Committee Political Director found dead in a hotel room in Little Rock, Arkansas September 24, 1992. Described by Clinton as a "dear friend and trusted advisor."

ED WILLEY - Clinton fund raiser-found dead November 30, 1993 deep in the woods in Virginia of a gunshot wound to the head. His death was ruled a suicide, Willey died on the same day his wife Kathleen Willey claimed that Bill Clinton groped her in the oval office in the White House. Ed Willey was involved in several Clinton fund raising events.

JERRY PARKS - Head of Clinton's gubernatorial security team in Little Rock. Parks was gunned down in his car at a deserted intersection outside Little Rock. Park's son said his father was building a dossier on Clinton. He allegedly threatened to reveal this information. After he died the files were mysteriously removed from his house.

JAMES BUNCH - Died from a gunshot suicide. He was reported to have a "black book" of people containing names of influential people who visited prostitutes in Texas and Arkansas.

AMES WILSON - Was found dead May 18, 1993 from an apparent hanging suicide. Wilson was reported to have ties to Whitewater.

KATHY FERGUSON - Ex-wife of Arkansas Trooper Danny Ferguson died in May, 1994 was found dead in her living room with a gunshot wound to her head. It was ruled a suicide even though there were several packed suitcases, as if she was going somewhere. Danny Ferguson was a co-defendant along with Bill Clinton in the Paula Corbin Jones lawsuit. She was reported a possible corroborating witness for Paula Jones case.

BILL SHELTON - Arkansas State Trooper and fiancé of Kathy Ferguson. Critical of the suicide ruling of his fiancé', he was found dead in June, 1994 of a gunshot wound also ruled a suicide at the gravesite of his fiancé.

GANDY BAUGH - Attorney for Clinton friend Dan Lassater died by jumping out a window of a tall building January 1, 1994. His client was a convicted drug distributor.

FLORENCE MARTIN -Accountant subcontractor for the CIA related to the Barry Seal Mena Airport drug smuggling case. He died of three gunshot wounds.

SUZANNE COLEMAN - Reportedly has an affair with Clinton when he was Arkansas Attorney General. She died of a gunshot wound to back of head, ruled a suicide. Was pregnant at the time her death.

PAULA GROBER - Clinton's speech interpreter for the deaf from 1978 until her death December 9, 1992. She died in a one car accident.

DANNY CASOLARO - Investigative reporter. He was investigating Mena airport and Arkansas Development Finance Authority. He slit his wrists, apparent suicide in the middle of his investigation.

PAUL WILCHER - Attorney investigating corruption at Mena Airport with Casolaro and the 1980 "October Surprise" was found dead on a toilet June 22, 1993 in his Washington DC Apartment. Had delivered report to Janet Reno 3 weeks before his death.

JON PARNELL WALKER - Whitewater Investigator for Resolution Trust Corporation. Walker jumped to his death from his Arlington, Virginia apartment balcony August 15, 1993. Was investigating Morgan Guarantee scandal

BARBARA WISE – A Commerce Department Staffer, he worked closely with Ron Brown and John Huang. The cause of death is unknown. Wise died November 29, 1996. Her bruised nude body was found locked in her office at the Department of Commerce.

CHARLES MEISSNER - Assistant Secretary of Commerce who gave John Huang special security clearance, died shortly thereafter in a small plane crash.

DR. STANLEY HEARD - Chair National Chiropractic Heath Care Advisory committee died with his attorney STEVE DICKSON in a small plane crash. Heard, in addition to serving on Clinton's advisory council personally treated Clinton's mother, stepfather and brother.

BARRY SEAL - drug running pilot out of Mena, Arkansas, Death was no accident.

JOHNNY LAWHON Jr. - Mechanic, found a check made out to Clinton in the trunk of a car left in his repair shop. He died when his car hit a utility pole.

STANLEY HUGGINS – Ruled a suicide. He had Investigated Madison Guarantee. His report was never released.

HERSHELL FRIDAY - Attorney & Clinton fund raiser died March 1, 1994 when his plane exploded.

KEVIN IVES & DON HENRY - Known as "The boys on the track" case. Reports say the boys may have stumbled upon the Mena Arkansas Airport Drug operation. This controversial case is where the initial report of death was due to falling asleep on railroad track. Later reports claim the two had been slain before being placed on the tracks. Many linked to the case died before their testimony could come before a Grand Jury.

The following six people were involved in the IVES/HENRY case.

KEITH CONEY - Died when his motorcycle slammed into the back of a truck in July, 1988.

KEITH McMASKLE - Died, stabbed 113 times, November 1988.

GREGORY COLLINS - Died from a gunshot wound, January 1989.

JEFF RHODES - He was shot, mutilated and found burned in a trash dump in April 1989.

JAMES MILAN - He was found decapitated.

JORDAN KETTLESON - Was found shot to death in the front seat of his pickup truck in June 1990.

RICHARD WINTERS - Winters was a suspect in the Ives/Henry deaths. He was killed in set-up robbery in July 1989.

The following are all former bodyguards of Bill Clinton.

MAJOR WILLIAM S. BARKLEY JR;

CAPTAIN SCOTT J. REYNOLDS;

SGT BRIAN HANEY;

SGT TIM SABEL;

MAJOR GENERAL WILLIAM ROBERTSON;

COL WILLIAM DENSBERGER;

COL ROBERT KELLY;

SPEC GARY RHODES;

STEVE WILLIS;

ROBERT WILLIAMS;

CONWAY LEBLEU;

TODD McKEEHAN.